HOW TO COPE

ANCIENT WISDOM FOR MODERN READERS

▪ ▪ ▪ ▪ ▪ ▪

For a full list of titles in the series, go to https://press.princeton.edu/series/ancient-wisdom-for-modern-readers.

How to Cope: An Ancient Guide to Enduring Hardship by Boethius

How to Be Caring: An Ancient Guide to a Compassionate Life by Shantideva

How to Make a Home: An Ancient Guide to Style and Comfort by Vitruvius and Guests

How to Have Willpower: An Ancient Guide to Not Giving In by Plutarch and Prudentius

How to Talk about Love: An Ancient Guide for Modern Relationships by Plato

How to Eat: An Ancient Guide for Healthy Living by a Buffet of Ancient Authors

How to Lose Yourself: An Ancient Guide to Letting Go by the Buddha and His Followers

How to Be Queer: An Ancient Guide to Sexuality by Sappho, Plato, and Other Lovers

How to Get Over a Breakup: An Ancient Guide to Moving On by Ovid

How to Make Money: An Ancient Guide to Wealth Management by Pliny & Co.

How to Focus: A Monastic Guide for an Age of Distraction by John Cassian

How to Be Healthy: An Ancient Guide to Wellness by Galen

How to Care about Animals: An Ancient Guide to Creatures Great and Small by Porphyry and Friends

How to Flourish: An Ancient Guide to Living Well by Aristotle

HOW TO COPE

■ ■ ■ ■ ■ ■

An Ancient Guide to Enduring Hardship

Boethius

Selections from

The Consolation of Philosophy

Selected, translated, and introduced

by Philip Freeman

PRINCETON UNIVERSITY PRESS

PRINCETON AND OXFORD

Published by Princeton University Press
41 William Street, Princeton, New Jersey 08540
99 Banbury Road, Oxford OX2 6JX

press.princeton.edu

GPSR Authorized Representative: Easy Access System Europe - Mustamäe tee 50, 10621 Tallinn, Estonia, gpsr.requests@easproject.com

ISBN 9780691259161
ISBN (e-book) 9780691259222

British Library Cataloging-in-Publication Data is available

Editorial: Rob Tempio and Chloe Coy
Production Editorial: Sara Lerner
Text and Jacket Design: Heather Hansen
Production: Erin Suydam
Publicity: William Pagdatoon and Charlotte Coyne
Jacket Credit: Adam Eastland / Alamy Stock Photo

This book has been composed in Stempel Garamond with Futura

Printed in the United States of America

1 3 5 7 9 10 8 6 4 2

CONTENTS

INTRODUCTION

What do you do when your life has fallen apart? This was the problem faced by a man named Boethius fifteen hundred years ago as he sat alone in a prison cell waiting to die.

Anicius Manlius Severinus Boethius was born in Italy around 480 CE, in the twilight years following the collapse of the western Roman Empire. Only four years earlier Odoacer, the Gothic king of Italy, had deposed the last Roman emperor in the West, a young man named Romulus Augustulus. But the old and noble Roman families, such as the one Boethius was born into, still enjoyed the wealth and privileges of the landed aristocracy, while the senate of Rome still met regularly in the Forum as it had for centuries. But the Roman world was only a shadow of what it once had been. The emperors still ruled what remained of the empire in the East from the new city of Constantinople, but Italy—along with Britain, Gaul, Spain, and parts of North Africa—had decades before fallen under the sway of invading Germanic tribes from the north. For

the most part these were not the destructive barbarian hordes of popular imagination, but instead organized bands of Christianized German warriors along with their followers and families who wanted to settle in Roman territory and peacefully rule their Roman subjects, who far outnumbered them, demanding only land and taxes for themselves. In Italy it was the Ostrogoths who reigned under their king Theoderic, who, with at least the tacit assent of Emperor Zeno in Constantinople, had killed Odoacer and taken control of the peninsula while Boethius was still a boy. Theoderic had been a royal hostage in Constantinople during his teenage years and was a faithful Christian of the Arian sect, which differed from the Catholic Romans of Italy in matters of Trinitarian theology. Nonetheless, the Arians of Theoderic's court in Ravenna and his Catholic subjects in Rome lived together amicably enough, though the Romans were ever wary of their warlike Gothic rulers, just as the Germans feared that the loyalty of their Roman subjects lay more with the distant emperor in Constantinople than with Theoderic.

Boethius's father had risen to the highest rank of Roman government as a consul, a largely ceremonial role at the time but still fiercely coveted by the noble families of Rome. When his father died while Boethius was young, he was adopted by an-

other leading Christian family headed by Quintus Symmachus, the leader of the senate in Rome and highly respected as both a government official and a scholar. Under the guidance of Symmachus, the precocious and brilliant young Boethius became a master of literature, philosophy, logic, music, astronomy, mathematics, science, and theology, as well as gaining a fluency in the Greek language that was becoming increasingly rare in Italy. He married Rusticiana, the daughter of Symmachus, further cementing his ties to the leading family of Rome. Boethius's talents attracted the attention of Theoderic, who asked him to construct a complicated water clock as a gift for the king of the Germanic Burgundians and to find the best lyre player in the land to send to the court of the Frankish ruler Clovis. Theoderic trusted and respected Boethius so much that he appointed him sole consul when he was only thirty and later selected him as *magister officiorum*—master of the offices—a position of tremendous responsibility that included supervision of the civil service and officials at Ravenna. Just over a decade after his own service as consul, Boethius's two sons were chosen by Theoderic as joint consuls, a moment Boethius confessed was the proudest of his life.

But Boethius always considered himself a scholar more than a government official. He loved the

Greek and Roman classics, especially the philosophical writings of Plato and Aristotle, who had lived nine centuries earlier. He translated many of Aristotle's works from Greek into Latin and made it his life's goal to make the complete writings of both philosophers available for his Roman countrymen. He also wrote several surviving treatises on Christian theology, including a defense of the orthodox view of the Trinity. Boethius's translations of Greek philosophical works would become standard texts in western Europe and in some cases the only means by which Greek philosophy would be known in the Latin Middle Ages.

But as Theoderic grew older and more suspicious of the loyalties of his Roman officials, Boethius was accused in a plot involving leading Roman citizens who had allegedly appealed to the emperor in Constantinople to side with them against the Ostrogothic ruler of Italy. Whether there was a basis in fact for this charge is debatable, but Boethius was nonetheless summarily condemned by Theoderic on the charge of treason and thrown into prison to await brutal torture and execution. It was during this time of imprisonment, as the reality of a painful death loomed ever before him, that Boethius turned for comfort and hope to earlier Greek and Roman writings and there in his cell composed his *Consolation of Philosophy*.

One important point to note about the *Consolation* is that it is not a Christian book. Boethius was certainly a Christian as seen in his works on theology, but in the *Consolation* he intentionally doesn't appeal to scripture or Christian tradition. The work relies largely on Stoic and Neoplatonic ideas to argue forcefully for a just universe and to declare that human free will and divine providence are not contradictory. But the God underlying the universe in the *Consolation* is the God of Plato, Aristotle, and Cicero, not of the Bible. This isn't to say that the *Consolation* opposes Christianity, simply that it deliberately uses the older Greek and Roman intellectual heritage to make its argument. Boethius indeed has long been criticized by some Christian authors as insufficiently orthodox or even as a secret pagan, but this is misunderstanding the intentions of the book. As C. S. Lewis said when he imagined what Boethius himself would say to such criticism: "But did you not read my title? I wrote philosophically, not religiously, because I had chosen the consolations of philosophy, not those of religion as my subject. You might as well ask why a book on arithmetic does not use geometrical methods."[1]

The *Consolation* has been tremendously popular and influential with readers since it was composed by Boethius over fifteen centuries ago. It

was required reading for any educated person in medieval Europe since the time of Charlemagne. King Alfred translated it into Old English, Chaucer turned it into Middle English, and Elizabeth I supposedly took only a day to translate it into the English of her time. Thomas Aquinas and Dante are just a few of the great writers who were deeply influenced by Boethius's work.

But Boethius is not a writer just for the past. His *Consolation of Philosophy* is a timeless classic of struggle with the most difficult issues of life for modern readers of any background. Few people will finish the book unmoved by the passion, courage, and remarkable vision of this last of the great Roman authors.

There are many lessons modern readers can learn from Boethius, even if they don't agree with everything he says. These include:

1. *Fortune is always changing.* Boethius calls fortune a wheel that is always turning. Good fortune will always be followed by bad and bad by good in turn. Whatever misfortune you're going through in your life won't last forever.
2. *Bad fortune is actually more beneficial for you than good fortune.* No one wants to

suffer, but hard times are when we grow as a person. As the ancient Greek poet Aeschylus put it: "Whoever learns must suffer. Even in our sleep, pain that cannot forget falls drop by drop upon the heart, and in our despair, against our will, wisdom comes to us."

3. *Hard times teach you who your true friends are*. Friends are easy to find when all is going well for you, but when things turn bad, fair-weather friends disappear. Only your true friends will remain by your side when your world comes crashing down.
4. *The things people often value the most do not bring true happiness*. Riches, honors, power, fame, and sensual pleasure are not evil in themselves, but if you think they will bring you lasting joy in your life you are fooling yourself. People in the world who have an abundance of such things can still feel very empty inside.
5. *The secret to true happiness lies in the pursuit of goodness*. Boethius uses the Latin word *virtus* ("virtue") to describe this quality that can free us from the wheel of fortune, though not in the prudish sense of abstaining from sensual pleasures. Boethius agrees with Aristotle that virtue is instead an

> activity of the soul searching for goodness. It isn't a matter of following a rulebook of things we shouldn't do but seeking and applying to our lives transcendent values that lie beyond ourselves.

We are fortunate that the text of the *Consolation of Philosophy* was spirited out of Boethius's prison cell before his death and survived the centuries to be copied repeatedly and read by later generations. Since it was a hugely popular book in medieval times throughout western Europe, we have hundreds of early manuscripts from which modern editors have carefully reconstructed the original text. My primary source has been the standard Latin edition of Ludwig Bieler (1984), but I have also drawn on the work of Sharples (1992) and Moreschini (2005).

For the sake of brevity, I have omitted all poems but the first of the *Consolation* along with the entire fifth book. In this final book Boethius discusses not the problem of misfortune in human life that is the subject of the rest of the volume but the related issue of free will and divine providence.

HOW TO COPE

ANICII MANLII SEVERINI BOETHII

PHILOSOPHIAE CONSOLATIONIS

THE CONSOLATION OF PHILOSOPHY

LIBER I

Carmina qui quondam studio florente peregi,
flebilis heu maestos cogor inire modos.
Ecce mihi lacerae dictant scribenda Camenae
et veris elegi fletibus ora rigant.

Has saltem nullus potuit pervincere terror,
ne nostrum comites prosequerentur iter.
Gloria felicis olim viridisque iuventae
solantur maesti nunc mea fata senis.
Venit enim properata malis inopina senectus
et dolor aetatem iussit inesse suam.
Intempestivi funduntur vertice cani
et tremit effeto corpore laxa cutis.
Mors hominum felix quae se nec dulcibus annis
inserit et maestis saepe vocata venit.

Eheu quam surda miseros avertitur aure
et flentes oculos claudere saeva negat.
Dum levibus male fida bonis fortuna faveret,
paene caput tristis merserat hora meum.

BOOK 1
A Visitor in Prison

I, who once wrote songs with joyful eagerness,
    alas, am now forced to sing sad verses with weeping.[1]
Behold, the Muses,[2] torn with grief, bid me write.
    And so these mournful verses wet my cheeks with
        honest tears.
No terror can discourage these ladies, at least,
    from coming as my companions on this journey.
They once were the glory of my green and happy youth,
    now in my sad old age they comfort me.[3]
For age has come unexpected, hastened by evils,
    and sorrow has added her years to mine.
My hair is too soon white upon my head
    and my skin hangs loose on my trembling body.
Happy is death when it thrusts itself upon us not in the
    sweet years,
    but comes instead to those wretches who call for it
        often.
Oh woe! It turns away with a deaf ear from the miserable
    and cruelly refuses to close my weeping eyes.
Once treacherous Fortune[4] favored me with passing joys,
    then the bitter hour came that bowed my head.

Nunc quia fallacem mutavit nubila vultum,
protrahit ingratas impia vita moras.
Quid me felicem totiens iactastis amici?
Qui cecidit, stabili non erat ille gradu.

Haec dum mecum tacitus ipse reputarem querimoniamque lacrimabilem stili officio signarem, adstitisse mihi supra verticem visa est mulier reverendi admodum vultus, oculis ardentibus et ultra communem hominum valentiam perspicacibus colore vivido atque inexhausti vigoris, quamvis ita aevi plena foret ut nullo modo nostrae crederetur aetatis, statura discretionis ambiguae. Nam nunc quidem ad communem sese hominum mensuram cohibebat, nunc vero pulsare caelum summi verticis cacumine videbatur; quae cum altius caput extulisset, ipsum etiam caelum penetrabat respicientiumque hominum frustrabatur intuitum.

Vestes erant tenuissimis filis subtili artificio, indissolubili materia perfectae quas, uti post eadem prodente cognovi, suis manibus ipsa texuerat. Quarum speciem, veluti fumosas imagines solet, caligo quaedam neglectae vetustatis obduxerat. Harum in extrema margine ·Π· Graecum, in supremo vero ·Θ·, legebatur intextum. Atque inter utrasque litteras in scalarum modum gradus quidam insigniti videbantur quibus ab inferiore ad superius elementum. esset

Now in darkness she has changed her deceitful face,
so that my cursed life drags on with unwelcome days.
Why, my friends, did you so often call me blessed?
The one who fell was never on solid ground.

While I was silently thinking these things to myself and writing down this tearful lament with the help of my pen, there seemed to stand above my head a woman, awe-inspiring in her appearance. Her eyes burned with fire and penetrated far beyond what is common for mortals. She had a vivid color and inexhaustible strength, yet she seemed so ancient I could scarcely believe she belonged to our age. Her height was hard to say, for sometimes she seemed to confine herself within ordinary human measure, but at other times she seemed to touch the sky with the top of her head. Then, when she lifted herself higher still, she seemed to break through the heavens and disappear beyond the sight of mortals.

Her clothing was made of the most delicate, imperishable material woven with great skill—I later learned, for she told me, that she had made it with her own hands. But a dark film from long neglect covered her clothes, as with smoky images.[5] On the bottom hem was woven the Greek letter *Pi*, while on the top of the garment was a *Theta*. Between the two letters was a ladder of steps rising from the lower to the higher, as if one might climb it.[6] This

ascensus. Eandem tamen vestem violentorum quorundam sciderant manus et particulas quas quisque potuit abstulerant. Et dextera quidem eius libellos, sceptrum vero sinistra gestabat.

Quae ubi poeticas Musas vidit nostro adsistentes toro fletibusque meis verba dictantes, commota paulisper ac torvis inflammata luminibus.

"Quis," inquit, "has scenicas meretriculas ad hunc aegrum permisit accedere quae dolores eius non modo nullis remediis foverent, verum dulcibus insuper alerent venenis? Hae sunt enim quae infructuosis affectuum spinis uberem fructibus rationis segetem necant hominumque mentes assuefaciunt morbo, non liberant. At si quem profanum, uti vulgo solitum vobis, blanditiae vestrae detraherent, minus moleste ferendum putarem; nihil quippe in eo nostrae operae laederentur. Hunc vero Eleaticis atque Academicis studiis innutritum? Sed abite potius Sirenes usque in exitium dulces meisque eum Musis curandum sanandumque relinquite."

His ille chorus increpitus deiecit humi maestior vultum confessusque rubore verecundiam limen tristis excessit. At ego cuius acies lacrimis mersa caligaret nec dinoscere possem quaenam haec esset mulier tam imperiosae auctoritatis, obstipui visuque in terram defixo quidnam deinceps esset actura,

same garment had been torn by the hands of violent men who each had carried off a scrap of cloth as they were able. In her right hand the lady carried books, but in her left she bore a scepter.

When she saw the Muses of poetry standing by my bed dictating words to accompany my tears, she grew angry for a moment and her eyes flashed with raging fire.

"Who," she said, "allowed these theatrical whores to visit this sick man? Not only have they no remedies for his pains, but their sweet poisons make it worse! These are the women who choke off the rich fruit of reason with barren thorns of emotion. They accustom the minds of mortals to sickness rather than curing them. If you were seducing some ordinary man with your empty lies as you usually do, it wouldn't matter so much to me. You wouldn't be hindering my work so much then. But this man was nourished on the teachings of Parmenides and Plato![7] Get out of here now, you Sirens,[8] you who so sweetly bring destruction to mortals! Leave him for *my* Muses to care for and make whole."

Shamed by her words, they hung their heads while their blushes confirmed the truth. In sorrow then they departed my room. But I—whose vision was so blinded by tears that I couldn't recognize this woman of such commanding authority—was struck dumb and lowered my eyes to the ground,

exspectare tacitus coepi. Tum illa propius accedens in extrema lectuli mei parte consedit meumque intuens vultum luctu gravem atque in humum maerore deiectum his versibus de nostrae mentis perturbatione conquesta est.

"Sed medicinae," inquit, "tempus est quam querelae."

Tum vero totis in me intenta luminibus:

"Tune ille es," ait, "qui nostro quondam lacte nutritus nostris educatus alimentis in virilis animi robur evaseras? Atqui talia contuleramus arma quae nisi prior abiecisses, invicta te firmitate tuerentur. Agnoscisne me? Quid taces? Pudore an stupore siluisti? Mallem pudore, sed te, ut video, stupor oppressit."

Cumque me non modo tacitum sed elinguem prorsus mutumque vidisset, admovit pectori meo leniter manum et: "Nihil," inquit, "pericli est; lethargum patitur communem inlusarum mentium morbum. Sui paulisper oblitus est; recordabitur facile, si quidem nos ante cognoverit. Quod ut possit,

waiting in silence for what she would do next. She came closer and sat on the edge of my bed. Then she gazed at my face, so worn with grief and cast down to the earth in sorrow. Sadly she began to mourn the confusion of my mind.

Do You Remember Me?

"But now is time for medicine," she said, "not complaining."

Then looking at me intently with her eyes, she said:

"Are you that man who once was nursed on my milk and nourished with my food until you grew into the full strength of your mind? And didn't I give you such weapons as would protect you even now, unconquered and steadfast, if you hadn't thrown them all away? Don't you recognize me? Why are you silent? Is it from shame or confusion? I would prefer it were shame, but, as I see now, it's confusion."

And when she saw that I was not only silent but completely speechless and unable to talk, she gently placed her hand on my chest and said: "There is no real danger here. He suffers only from forgetfulness, a common disease of deceived minds. He has forgotten for a little while who he is. He will

paulisper lumina eius mortalium rerum nube caligantia tergamus."

Haec dixit oculosque meos fletibus undantes contracta in rugam veste siccavit.

Haud aliter tristitiae nebulis dissolutis hausi caelum et ad cognoscendam medicantis faciem mentem recepi. Itaque ubi in eam deduxi oculos intuitumque defixi, respicio nutricem meam cuius ab adulescentia laribus obversatus fueram Philosophiam.

"Et quid," inquam, "tu in has exilii nostri solitudines, o omnium magistra virtutum, supero cardine delapsa venisti? An ut tu quoque mecum rea falsis criminationibus agiteris?"

"An," inquit illa, "te alumne desererem nec sarcinam quam mei nominis invidia sustulisti, communicate tecum labore partirer? Atqui Philosophiae fas non erat incomitatum relinquere iter innocentis; meam scilicet criminationem vererer et quasi novum aliquid acciderit, perhorrescerem? Nunc enim primum censes apud inprobos mores lacessitam periculis esse sapientiam? Nonne apud

remember[9] easily enough, for he knew me once before. And so that he might remember, let's clear away for a time that blinding cloud of worldly cares from his eyes."[10]

Saying this, she gathered together the folds of her robe and wiped away the tears filling my eyes.

Recognition at Last

In this same way the clouds of my misery were scattered and I drank in the light. Then my memory returned enough to recognize the face of the one who healed me. When I turned my eyes to her and looked closely, I saw my nurse in whose home I had dwelled since my youth—Philosophy.

"Why," I said, "have you, teacher of all virtues, come down from the heights of heaven to my lonely place of exile? Are you here to suffer false accusations along with me?"

"Would I desert you, my child?" she replied. "Wouldn't I share with you this labor and burden you bear because of the hatred of my name? Is it right that Philosophy abandon an innocent man to walk his path alone? Did you really believe I would fear an accusation against me, as if that were something new? Did you think this was the first time wisdom has been threatened with danger from those

veteres quoque ante nostri Platonis aetatem magnum saepe certamen cum stultitiae temeritate certavimus eodemque superstite praeceptor eius Socrates iniustae victoriam mortis me adstante promeruit? Cuius hereditatem cum deinceps Epicureum vulgus ac Stoicum ceterique pro sua quisque parte raptum ire molirentur meque reclamantem renitentemque velut in partem praedae traherent, vestem quam meis texueram manibus, disciderunt abreptisque ab ea panniculis totam me sibi cessisse credentes abiere. In quibus quoniam quaedam nostri habitus vestigia videbantur, meos esse familiares inprudentia rata nonnullus eorum profanae multitudinis errore pervertit.

Quod si nec Anaxagorae fugam nec Socratis venenum nec Zenonis tormenta quoniam sunt peregrina novisti, at Canios, at Senecas, at Soranos quorum nec pervetusta nec incelebris memoria est, scire potuisti. Quos nihil aliud in cladem detraxit nisi quod nostris moribus instituti studiis improborum dissimillimi videbantur. Itaque nihil est quod admirere, si in hoc vitae salo circumflantibus agitemur procellis, quibus hoc maxime propositum est pessimi displicere. Quorum quidem tametsi est numerosus exercitus, spernendus tamen est, quoniam nullo duce regitur, sed errore tantum temere

of wicked ways? Didn't I in ancient days, before the time of my beloved Plato, often join in fierce battle against arrogant stupidity? And although Plato survived, his teacher Socrates won the victory of an unjust death while I stood by his side.[11] Afterward the crowds of Epicureans and Stoics[12] and the rest each in their own way tried to seize his legacy for themselves and so carried me away shouting and struggling as if I were part of their plunder. They tore at parts of the robe I had woven with my own hands, thinking as they went away that they had somehow obtained all there was of me. Since they were seen with some little scraps of my clothing, they were foolishly thought to be my companions and many of them were corrupted by the errors of the ignorant mob.

"But even if you don't know about the flight of Anaxagoras, the poisoning of Socrates, or the torture of Zeno—they did happen in foreign lands after all—surely you can recall those like Canius, Seneca, and Soranus whose memory is neither ancient nor obscure.[13] The only reason they died was that they were devoted to my cause and were seen as utterly disinterested in the ways of evil. And so you shouldn't be surprised if we are tossed about on the seas of this life by storms blowing from all directions when our greatest goal is to displease wicked men. For even if their army is numerous,

ac passim lymphante raptatur. Qui si quando contra nos aciem struens valentior incubuerit, nostra quidem dux copias suas in arcem contrahit, illi vero circa diripiendas inutiles sarcinulas occupantur. At nos desuper inridemus vilissima rerum quaeque rapientes securi totius furiosi tumultus eoque vallo muniti quo grassanti stultitiae adspirare fas non sit.

"Sentisne," inquit, "haec atque animo inlabuntur tuo, an ὄνος λύρας?[14] Quid fles, quid lacrimis manas? Ἐξαύδα, μὴ κεῦθε νόῳ. Si operam medicantis exspectas, oportet vulnus detegas."

Tum ego collecto in vires animo: "Anne adhuc eget admonitione nec per se satis eminet fortunae in nos saevientis asperitas? Nihilne te ipsa loci facies movet? Haecine est bibliotheca, quam certissimam tibi sedem nostris in laribus ipsa delegeras? In qua mecum saepe residens de humanarum divinarumque rerum scientia disserebas? Talis habitus talisque vultus erat, cum tecum naturae secreta rimarer,

we should hold them in contempt, for they are led by no general, rushing here and there as they are driven about by foolish error. And if ever their army attacks us with all their might, our leader withdraws her forces into her own citadel, leaving the enemy to busy themselves plundering our useless baggage. We look down on them and laugh while they grab at everything of least value, while we are safe behind a wall that cannot be scaled by such raging stupidity.

The Complaints of Boethius

"Do you understand what I'm saying to you?" she asked. "Have my words made their way into your head? Or are you like the donkey hearing a lyre?[15] Why are you crying? Why are your cheeks covered with tears? As Homer says, 'Speak up, don't hide what's on your mind.'[16] If you want a doctor to treat you, you first must uncover your wound."

So I gathered up my courage to its full strength and spoke to her: "Do I really need to explain to you even now how savage the attack of Fortune has been against me? Isn't the cause of my pain obvious to you? Does this look like the library in my house which you yourself chose as your constant dwelling place? Isn't that where you would sit with me and talk about the knowledge of things both human and

cum mihi siderum vias radio describeres, cum mores nostros totiusque vitae rationem ad caelestis ordinis exempla formares? Haecine praemia referimus tibi obsequentes?

"Atqui tu hanc sententiam Platonis ore sanxisti: beatas fore res publicas, si eas vel studiosi sapientiae regerent vel earum rectores studere sapientiae contigisset. Tu eiusdem viri ore hanc sapientibus capessendae rei publicae necessariam causam esse monuisti, ne improbis flagitiosisque civibus urbium relicta gubernacula pestem bonis ac perniciem ferrent.

"Hanc igitur auctoritatem secutus quod a te inter secreta otia didiceram transferre in actum publicae administrationis optavi. Tu mihi et qui te sapientium mentibus inseruit deus conscii nullum me ad magistratum nisi commune bonorum omnium studium detulisse. Inde cum inprobis graves inexorabilesque discordiae et quod conscientiae libertas habet, pro tuendo iure spreta potentiorum semper offensio.

"Quotiens ego Conigastum in inbecilli cuiusque fortunas impetum facientem obvius excepi, quotiens

divine? Did my clothes or face look like this when I used to probe the secrets of nature with you or when you traced the path of the stars for me with your measuring rod or when you shaped my very reasoning and the course of my whole life according to the heavenly order? Is *this* how you reward those who follow you?

"Aren't you the one who decreed through the words of Plato that blessed is the state ruled by philosophers or by rulers who love wisdom?[17] You warned us through the words of that same man that this is why those devoted to wisdom should enter into political life—to prevent power from falling into the hands of wicked and unprincipled men and so bring ruin and disaster on the good.

"That is why, following your own command, I chose to devote myself to public service and make use of what I learned from you during our quiet hours together. You and the God who planted you in the minds of the wise are my witnesses that I had no other motivation for entering political life than a desire to benefit all good people. But because of this I have faced bitter and relentless conflict with the wicked. And because of my freedom of conscience and upholding of the law, I have faced the constant anger of those more powerful than me.

"How many times did I confront Conigastus when he was trying to steal the wealth of some

Trigguillam regiae praepositum domus ab incepta, perpetrata iam prorsus iniuria deieci, quotiens miseros quos infinitis calumniis inpunita barbarorum semper avaritia vexabat, obiecta periculis auctoritate protexi! Numquam me ab iure ad iniuriam quisquam detraxit.

"Provincialium fortunas tum privatis rapinis tum publicis vectigalibus pessumdari non aliter quam qui patiebantur indolui. Cum acerbae famis tempore gravis atque inexplicabilis indicta coemptio profligatura inopia Campaniam provinciam videretur, certamen adversum praefectum praetorii communis commodi ratione suscepi, rege cognoscente contendi et ne coemptio exigeretur, evici.

"Paulinum consularem virum cuius opes Palatinae canes iam spe atque ambitione devorassent, ab ipsis hiantium faucibus traxi. Ne Albinum consularem virum praeiudicatae accusationis poena corriperet, odiis me Cypriani delatoris opposui.

"Satisne in me magnas videor exacervasse discordias? Sed esse apud ceteros tutior debui qui mihi

powerless man? How often did I stop Trigguilla, who was in charge of the king's household, when he planned to commit some injustice—or even when he already had?[18] How often did I protect some unfortunate soul from the greed of the barbarians (who were never punished) even though using my authority put me in danger? Never has anyone turned me away from justice toward injustice.

"When the estates of families in the provinces were devastated first by greedy individuals and then by state taxation, I grieved as much as those who suffered these injustices. When in a time of terrible famine, a ruinous and indefensible forced sale of grain[19] was imposed on Campania that would have pushed the province into destitution, I took up the fight against the Praetorian prefect for the good of all. I argued before the king himself against the enforcement of this edict—and I won.[20]

"I rescued the former consul Paulinus from the very jaws of the palace dogs who would have devoured him, as they had already devoured his wealth in their ambitious greed. And then to keep Albinus, also a former consul, safe from the judgment of those who would have condemned him without trial, I earned the hatred of his accuser Cyprian.[21]

"Doesn't it seem like I have stirred up enough raging anger against myself? But shouldn't I in doing so have made myself more secure among

amore iustitiae nihil apud aulicos quo magis essem tutior reservavi.

"Quibus autem deferentibus perculsi sumus? Quorum Basilius olim regio ministerio depulsus in delationem nostri nominis alieni aeris necessitate compulsus est. Opilionem vero atque Gaudentium cum ob innumeras multiplicesque fraudes ire in exilium regia censura decrevisset cumque illi parere nolentes sacrarum sese aedium defensione tuerentur compertumque id regi foret, edixit: uti ni intra praescriptum diem Ravenna urbe decederent, notas insigniti frontibus pellerentur. Quid huic severitati posse astrui videtur? Atqui in eo die deferentibus eisdem nominis nostri delatio suscepta est. Quid igitur? Nostraene artes ita meruerunt? An illos accusatores iustos fecit praemissa damnatio? Itane nihil fortunam puduit si minus accusatae innocentiae, at accusantium vilitatis?

"At cuius criminis arguimur summam quaeris? Senatum dicimur salvum esse voluisse. Modum desideras? Delatorem ne documenta deferret quibus senatum maiestatis reum faceret impedisse criminamur.

those outside the royal court[22] since my love of justice caused me to show no favor to those at court to make myself safer there?

"Who are the informers then who have brought me low? One was Basilius, a man previously dismissed from royal service, who was forced to denounce me because of his debts. Then there were Opilio and Gaudentius.[23] A decree had gone out from the king sentencing them both to exile for their countless frauds, but they sought sanctuary in a holy temple.[24] When the king found out, he ordered them to leave Ravenna before the appointed day or else have brands burned into their foreheads and then be driven from the city. What could be a harsher acknowledgment of their guilt than that? Yet on that very day those same men made an accusation against me and their denunciation was accepted. Tell me, did my actions merit that? Did my prearranged conviction somehow turn these accusers into just men? Shouldn't Fortune have been ashamed, if not because an innocent man was accused then at least because the accusers were so vile?

"Do you want to know what the heart of the accusation against me is? It's that I desired the safety of the Senate. And do you want to know how I did that? By trying to prevent an informer from bringing forward documents claiming the Senate was guilty of treason.

"Quid igitur, o magistra, censes? Infitiabimur crimen, ne tibi pudor simus? At volui nec umquam velle desistam. Fatebimur? Sed impediendi delatoris opera cessavit. An optasse illius ordinis salutem nefas vocabo? Ille quidem suis de me decretis, uti hoc nefas esset, effecerat. Sed sibi semper mentiens inprudentia rerum merita non potest inmutare nec mihi Socratico decreto fas esse arbitror vel occuluisse veritatem vel concessisse mendacium. Verum id quoquo modo sit, tuo sapientiumque iudicio aestimandum relinquo. Cuius rei seriem atque veritatem, ne latere posteros queat, stilo etiam memoriaeque mandavi.

"Nam de compositis falso litteris quibus libertatem arguor sperasse Romanam quid attinet dicere? Quarum fraus aperta patuisset, si nobis ipsorum confessione delatorum, quod in omnibus negotiis maximas vires habet, uti licuisset. Nam quae sperari reliqua libertas potest? Atque utinam posset ulla! Respondissem Canii verbo, qui cum a Gaio Caesare Germanici filio conscius contra se factae coniurationis fuisse diceretur: 'Si ego,' inquit, 'scissem, tu nescisses.'

"And so, my teacher, what do you think? Should I deny the charge to avoid causing you shame? But I *did* want the Senate to be safe and I always will. Should I confess then? But the effort to stop the informer has ended. Shall I say instead it was wrong to want to protect the Senate? Indeed, the Senate by its own decree against me has declared it wrong.[25] But such foolishness, always lying to itself, cannot change the merit of anything. I must follow the teaching of Socrates to neither hide the truth nor be a party to falsehood.[26] But I leave it to your judgment and that of other wise people to decide what is right. I have recorded with my pen the truth of this whole matter and the sequence of events so that they might be remembered and not forgotten by future generations.

"And concerning those false letters in which I supposedly argued for the freedom of the Roman people, what more is there to say? It would have been obvious they were frauds if I had been allowed to use the confessions of my accusers—always the most powerful defense in such matters. But what liberty can be hoped for now? How I wish there were some hope. If so I would have responded using the same words as Canius, who when Caligula accused him of participating in a plot against him said, 'If *I* had known about it, *you* would not.'

"Qua in re non ita sensus nostros maeror hebetavit ut impios scelerata contra virtutem querar molitos, sed quae speraverint effecisse vehementer admiror. Nam deteriora velle nostri fuerit fortasse defectus, posse contra innocentiam, quae sceleratus quisque conceperit inspectante deo, monstri simile est. Unde haud iniuria tuorum quidam familiarium quaesivit: 'Si quidem deus,' inquit, 'est, unde mala? Bona vero unde, si non est?'

"Sed fas fuerit nefarios homines qui bonorum omnium totiusque senatus sanguinem petunt, nos etiam quos propugnare bonis senatuique viderant, perditum ire voluisse. Sed num idem de patribus quoque merebamur? Meministi, ut opinor, quoniam me dicturum quid facturumve praesens semper ipsa dirigebas, meministi inquam, Veronae cum rex avidus exitii communis maiestatis crimen in Albinum delatae ad cunctum senatus ordinem transferre moliretur, universi innocentiam senatus quanta mei periculi securitate defenderim. Scis me haec et vera proferre et in nulla umquam mei laude iactasse. Minuit enim quodam modo se probantis conscientiae secretum, quotiens ostentando quid factum recipit famae pretium.

"In all this my wits are not so dulled by grief that I merely whine about wicked men seeking to do evil deeds against the good. What astounds me is that they actually get what they wish for. We may grant that it's a common human failing to have evil desires, but for every evil man to be able to carry out his plans against the innocent while God looks on is simply monstrous. It's not without reason that one of your followers wondered: 'If God exists, where does evil come from? But then, where does good come from if he doesn't?'[27]

"It is understandable if wicked men who seek the blood of all good people and the Senate should seek to destroy me too, since they saw me fighting for good men and for the Senate. But surely I didn't deserve the same treatment from the senators themselves! You'll remember, I think—since you were always by my side directing me whenever I was about to say or do anything—again I say you'll remember that when at Verona[28] the king, who was eager to destroy the whole Senate, tried to expand the charge of treason against Albinus to include all the senators, I defended the innocence of the whole Senate with no thought for my own safety. You know that I am speaking the truth, since in no way do I ever try to praise myself. For whenever someone boasts of what he did and earns some reward, by that much

"Sed innocentiam nostram quis exceperit eventus vides; pro verae virtutis praemiis falsi sceleris poenas subimus. Et cuius umquam facinoris manifesta confessio ita iudices habuit in severitate concordes ut non aliquos vel ipse ingenii error humani vel fortunae condicio cunctis mortalibus incerta submitteret? Si inflammare sacras aedes voluisse, si sacerdotes impio iugulare gladio, si bonis omnibus necem struxisse diceremur, praesentem tamen sententia, confessum tamen convictumve punisset. Nunc quingentis fere passuum milibus procul muti atque indefensi ob studium propensius in senatum morti proscriptionique damnamur. O meritos de simili crimine neminem posse convinci!

"Cuius dignitatem reatus ipsi etiam qui detulere viderunt, quam uti alicuius sceleris admixtione fuscarent, ob ambitum dignitatis sacrilegio me conscientiam polluisse mentiti sunt. Atqui et tu insita nobis omnem rerum mortalium cupidinem de nostri animi sede pellebas et sub tuis oculis sacrilegio locum esse fas non erat. Instillabas enim auribus cogitationibusque cotidie meis Pythagoricum illud:

in praising himself he diminishes the hidden benefits to his conscience.

"But now you see the result of my innocence. Instead of a reward for true virtue, I am punished for a crime I didn't commit. And in what sort of crime did even a full confession ever merit judges so united in their severity that none of them could be swayed by the fallibility of human nature or by the unpredictability of Fortune common to all mortals? If I had been accused of burning down holy temples or slitting the throats of priests with an unholy sword or plotting the slaughter of all good citizens, I would have at least been allowed to be present at my sentencing after I had confessed or been convicted. But here I am nearly five hundred miles away,[29] silenced and unable to defend myself, condemned to death and my property confiscated, all for being too zealous in my support of the Senate. How they richly deserve that no one else will ever be convicted on a similar charge!

"Even those who invented this accusation could see the dignity it gave me, and so to blacken my standing they lyingly added the wicked claim that in my ambition for high office I had defiled myself by indulging in sorcery.[30] But you yourself dwell deep within my spirit and have driven out any desire for earthly things. Under your gaze there is certainly no place for unholy arts. For you instilled every day

ἕπου θεῷ. Nec conveniebat vilissimorum me spirituum praesidia captare quem tu in hanc excellentiam componebas ut consimilem deo faceres. Praeterea penetral innocens domus, honestissimorum coetus amicorum, socer etiam sanctus et aeque ac tu ipsa reverendus ab omni nos huius criminis suspitione defendunt.

"Sed, o nefas, illi vero de te tanti criminis fidem capiunt atque hoc ipso videbimur affines fuisse maleficio, quod tuis inbuti disciplinis, tuis instituti moribus sumus. Ita non est satis nihil mihi tuam profuisse reverentiam, nisi ultro tu mea potius offensione lacereris.

"At vero hic etiam nostris malis cumulus accedit, quod existimatio plurimorum non rerum merita sed fortunae spectat eventum eaque tantum iudicat esse provisa quae felicitas commendaverit. Quo fit ut existimatio bona prima omnium deserat infelices. Qui nunc populi rumores, quam dissonae multiplicesque sententiae, piget reminisci. Hoc tantum dixerim ultimam esse adversae fortunae sarcinam, quod dum miseris aliquod crimen affingitur, quae perferunt meruisse creduntur. Et ego quidem bonis omnibus pulsus, dignitatibus exutus,

into my ears and mind that saying of Pythagoras: 'Follow God.'[31] It would not at all be appropriate for me to seek the help of the vilest of spirits when you raised me up in excellence to become like God. Beyond this, my blameless life in the sanctuary of my home, my companionship with the most honorable of friends, my father-in-law (a man as worthy of reverence as you) all defend me from any suspicion of this charge.

"But—and, oh, this is evil—those accusers gain credibility for their unholy charge because you and I seem in this supposed sorcery[32] to be allies, since I am so deeply immersed in your teachings and established in your ways.[33] And so it isn't enough that my reverence for you has done me no good, but now you too are being torn apart because of the attack on me.

"To add to all my troubles is the fact that the opinion of most people isn't formed by the merit of a case but by how chance makes it unfold. They judge that things turn out well for us only when we have acted rightly. Thus it is the good reputation we have in the eyes of everyone that vanishes first. It pains me to think about the rumors that are spreading about me now and how varied and contradictory popular opinion must be. I would say the ultimate burden of misfortune is that wretched people are believed to deserve what they suffer, even

existimatione foedatus ob beneficium supplicium tuli.

"Videre autem videor nefarias sceleratorum officinas gaudio laetitiaque fluitantes, perditissimum quemque novis delationum fraudibus imminentem, iacere bonos nostri discriminis terrore prostratos, flagitiosum quemque ad audendum quidem facinus impunitate, ad efficiendum vero praemiis incitari, insontes autem non modo securitate, verum ipsa etiam defensione privates.

Haec ubi continuato dolore delatravi, illa vultu placido nihilque meis questibus mota.

"Cum te," inquit, "maestum lacrimantemque vidissem, ilico miserum exsulemque cognovi. Sed quam id longinquum esset exilium, nisi tua prodidisset oratio, nesciebam. Sed tu quam procul a patria non quidem pulsus es sed aberrasti; ac si te pulsum existimari mavis, te potius ipse pepulisti. Nam id quidem de te numquam cuiquam fas fuisset.

when the charges against them are baseless. And so it is with me, deprived of my possessions, stripped of my honors, my reputation in ruins. I am punished for having done good.

"I seem to see the evil workshops of wicked men overflowing with joy and happiness. I see every scoundrel threatening new false denunciations. I see good people cast down on the ground trembling at what has happened to me. I see all the criminals encouraged to commit wicked deeds without fear of punishment and indeed encouraged by rewards to do them. All this has happened while the innocent are deprived not only of their safety but also of their defense."

A Prayer and a Response

While I was bawling all this out in continual lament,[34] Philosophy looked on me with a serene face, unmoved by my complaints.

Then she spoke: "When I saw you grief-stricken and full of tears, I knew immediately that you were a pitiable exile, but until you began to speak I had no idea how distant your banishment was. How far from your homeland you are! But you have not been expelled—no, you have wandered off all on your own. If you prefer to think that you have been

Si enim cuius oriundus sis patriae reminiscare, non uti Atheniensium quondam multitudinis imperio regitur, sed εἷς κοίρανός ἐστιν, εἷς βασιλεύς qui frequentia civium non depulsione laetetur; cuius agi frenis atque obtemperare iustitiae summa libertas est. An ignoras illam tuae civitatis antiquissimam legem, qua sanctum est ei ius exulare non esse quisquis in ea sedem fundare maluerit? Nam qui vallo eius ac munimine continetur, nullus metus est ne exul esse mereatur. At quisquis eam inhabitare velle desierit, pariter desinit etiam mereri.

"Itaque non tam me loci huius quam tua facies movet nec bibliothecae potius comptos ebore ac vitro parietes quam tuae mentis sedem requiro, in qua non libros sed id quod libris pretium facit, librorum quondam meorum sententias, collocavi.

"Et tu quidem de tuis in commune bonum meritis vera quidem, sed pro multitudine gestorum tibi pauca dixisti. De obiectorum tibi vel honestate vel falsitate cunctis nota memorasti. De sceleribus fraudibusque delatorum recte tu quidem strictim attingendum putasti, quod ea melius uberiusque recognoscentis omnia vulgi ore celebrentur. Increpuisti

exiled, then it is rather you who have exiled yourself, for no one else has that kind of power over you. Do you even remember your own homeland? It is not ruled by the decisions of the multitude as Athens once was, but in that place 'there is one commander, one king'[35] who delights in the company of his subjects, not in driving them out. To be led by his hand and to submit yourself to his justice is the highest liberty.[36] Do you not know the most ancient law of your city, the law that says anyone who has chosen to make his home there can never be banished? The one who lives within the walls and fortifications of that city need not fear that he will ever merit exile. But anyone who no longer wishes to live there ceases to deserve such assurance.

"And so it isn't the look of this place that moves me so much as your own appearance. I don't need a library decorated with ivory and glass as much as I do a seat in your mind. That is where I have stored up not books but that which gives books their value—the ideas of mine that they contain.

"You have spoken rightly about your services for the common good, and indeed you could have said much more. You have talked about the truthfulness—or rather untruthfulness—of all the charges brought against you. And you were right that you only needed to touch briefly on the wicked crimes and lies of those who accused you, since they are

etiam vehementer iniusti factum senatus. De nostra etiam criminatione doluisti, laesae quoque opinionis damna flevisti. Postremus adversum fortunam dolor incanduit conquestusque non aequa meritis praemia pensari, in extremo Musae saevientis, uti quae caelum terras quoque pax regeret, vota posuisti.

"Sed quoniam plurimus tibi affectuum tumultus incubuit diversumque te dolor, ira, maeror distrahunt, uti nunc mentis es, nondum te validiora remedia contingunt. Itaque lenioribus paulisper utemur, ut quae in tumorem perturbationibus influentibus induruerunt, ad acrioris vim medicaminis recipiendum tactu blandiore mollescant.

"Primum igitur paterisne me pauculis rogationibus statum tuae mentis attingere atque temptare, ut qui modus sit tuae curationis intellegam?"

"Tu vero arbitratu," inquam, "tuo quae voles ut responsurum rogato."

told better and more fully by the common crowd, who always find out about everything. You have also bemoaned passionately the injustice of the Senate. And of course you lamented the charges made against me and wept for the damage done to my reputation. Finally your anger burned brightly against unjust Fortune and you railed against rewards not being equal to merits. And then at the end of your raging verses you wished for the peace that rules the heavens to reign on earth as well.

"Since such a storm of passions has besieged you and since grief, anger, and sorrow are dragging you in different directions—for that is the sorry state of mind you are in—you can't yet be given stronger medicines. Thus for a time I will use gentler remedies so that your tumorous wound, swollen hard from confusing emotions rushing in, might soften by my touch and make you ready to accept more powerful treatments.

Gentle Medicine

"Will you first allow me to ask a few questions to examine[37] and test your state of mind, so that I might judge what cure is best for you?"

"Ask what you think is best," I said, "and I will answer whatever you wish."

Tum illa: "Huncine," inquit, "mundum temerariis agi fortuitisque casibus putas, an ullum credis ei regimen inesse rationis?"

"Atqui," inquam, "nullo existimaverim modo ut fortuita temeritate tam certa moveantur, verum operi suo conditorem praesidere deum scio nec umquam fuerit dies qui me ab hac sententiae veritate depellat."

"Ita est," inquit. "Nam id etiam paulo ante cecinisti, hominesque tantum divinae exsortes curae esse deplorasti. Nam de ceteris quin ratione regerentur, nihil movebare. Papae autem! Vehementer admiror cur in tam salubri sententia locatus aegrotes. Verum altius perscrutemur; nescio quid abesse coniecto. Sed dic mihi, quoniam ⟨a⟩ deo mundum regi non ambigis, quibus etiam gubernaculis regatur advertis?"

"Vix," inquam, "rogationis tuae sententiam nosco, nedum ad inquisita respondere queam."

"Num me," inquit, "fefellit abesse aliquid, per quod, velut hiante valli robore, in animum tuum perturbationum morbus inrepserit? Sed dic mihi, meministine, quis sit rerum finis, quove totius naturae tendat intentio?"

"Do you think," she asked, "that this world is ruled by random and chance events or do you believe some reason guides it?"

"There is no way," I said, "that I would ever believe this world of such order is governed by random chance. Indeed I know that God the creator presides over his own work. There will never come a day when I will believe this is not the truth."

"Yes," she replied, "this is what you were saying just a little while ago when you deplored that humans alone are not under divine care. Concerning the rest of the world, you had no doubt at all that they were governed by reason. How strange! I'm amazed that you are sick at all given your grounding in such a healthy belief. Truly we must examine this more deeply. I think there is something missing here. Tell me, since you don't doubt that the world is ruled by God, what do you think are the means by which he guides it?"[38]

"I can hardly understand your question," I said, "much less answer it."

"So I wasn't deceived, was I," she said, "in thinking something was missing? It's as if some disease had crept into your troubled mind as through a crack in a strong wall. But tell me, if you remember, what is the end of all things, the goal to which all nature strives?"

"Audieram," inquam, "sed memoriam maeror hebetavit."

"Atqui scis unde cuncta processerint?"

"Novi," inquam, deumque esse respondi.

"Et qui fieri potest, ut principio cognito quis sit rerum finis ignores? Verum hi perturbationum mores, ea valentia est, ut movere quidem loco hominem possint, convellere autem sibique totum exstirpare non possint. Sed hoc quoque respondeas velim, hominemne te essemeministi?"

"Quidni," inquam, "meminerim?"

"Quid igitur homo sit, poterisne proferre?"

"Hocine interrogas an esse me sciam rationale animal atque mortale? Scio et id me esse confiteor."

Et illa: "Nihilne aliud te esse novisti?"

"Nihil."

"Iam scio," inquit, "morbi tui aliam vel maximam causam; quid ipse sis, nosse desisti. Quare plenissime vel aegritudinis tuae rationem vel aditum reconciliandae sospitatis inveni. Nam quoniam tui oblivione confunderis, et exsulem te et exspoliatum propriis bonis esse doluisti. Quoniam vero quis sit rerum finis ignoras, nequam homines atque nefarios

"I heard it once," I replied, "but grief has blunted my memory."

"Do you know then the source from which all things come?"

"I know," I said and answered that it was God.

"And how can it be that you know the beginning of things but not their end? Indeed this is the power of confusing emotions, that they're able to move a man from his position but aren't able to knock him down completely and uproot him from himself. But answer me this—do you remember that you're a human being?"

"How could I not remember that?"

"And what is a human being? Are you able to say?"

"Are you asking me if I know I'm a rational and mortal animal? Yes, I do know it and admit that's what I am."

Then she asked, "Are you sure that you're nothing more?"

"Nothing."

"Now I know the other and most serious cause of your disease. You have forgotten what you are. Now I know fully the reason for your illness and the remedy to restore you to health. Because you are so confused by forgetfulness, you lamented that you were an exile and have lost all of your goods. And because you don't know the end and purpose of

potentes felicesque arbitraris. Quoniam vero quibus gubernaculis mundus regatur oblitus es, has fortunarum vices aestimas sine rectore fluitare—magnae non ad morbum modo verum ad interitum quoque causae. Sed sospitatis auctori grates, quod te nondum totum natura destituit.

"Habemus maximum tuae fomitem salutis veram de mundi gubernatione sententiam, quod eam non casuum temeritati sed divinae rationi subditam credis. Nihil igitur pertimescas; iam tibi ex hac minima scintillula vitalis calor inluxerit. Sed quoniam firmioribus remediis nondum tempus est et eam mentium constat esse naturam, ut quotiens abiecerint veras falsis opinionibus induantur ex quibus orta perturbationum caligo verum illum confundit intuitum, hanc paulisper lenibus mediocribusque fomentis attenuare temptabo, ut dimotis fallacium affectionum tenebris splendorem verae lucis possis agnoscere."

things, you think that wicked people are powerful and happy. And finally because you have forgotten by what means the world is controlled, you think that the ups and downs of Fortune happen without anyone guiding events. These problems are great enough to cause not only disease but even death. Still, you should give thanks to the author of health that your true nature has not yet abandoned you.

"We still have the best kindling for your health—your true opinion about the governance of the world, for you believe it is ruled not by random chance but by divine reason. So do not be afraid. Soon this tiny spark of life-giving heat will burst into flame. But since it's not yet time for stronger remedies and since it is the nature of the mind to clothe itself in false beliefs when it has abandoned true ones, I will try for a little while to clear away this fog with milder and gentler medicines, so that with the shadows of false beliefs driven away, you will be able to see the glory of true light."

INCIPIT LIBER II

Post haec paulisper obticuit atque ubi attentionem meam modesta taciturnitate collegit, sic exorsa est.

"Si penitus aegritudinis tuae causas habitumque cognovi, fortunae prioris affectu desiderioque tabescis. Ea tantum animi tui sicuti tu tibi fingis mutata pervertit. Intellego multiformes illius prodigii fucos et eo usque cum his quos eludere nititur blandissimam familiaritatem, dum intolerabili dolore confundat quos insperata reliquerit. Cuius si naturam mores ac meritum reminiscare, nec habuisse te in ea pulchrum aliquid nec amisisse cognosces, sed ut arbitror haud multum tibi haec in memoriam revocare laboraverim.

"Solebas enim praesentem quoque blandientemque virilibus incessere verbis eamque de nostro adyto prolatis insectabare sententiis. Verum omnis

BOOK 2

Fortune Is Never Constant

After this she was quiet for a little while. And when she had gained my attention by her modest silence, she began to speak:

"If I have properly understood the causes and the nature of your sickness, you are wasting away from a desire and longing for your previously happy condition. The changes caused by Fortune are the source of your deeply troubled mind—or at least that's how it seems to you. But I understand the many tricks[1] of that monster Fortune and the charming friendliness she shows to those she wishes to deceive, at least until she abandons them unexpectedly and leaves them confused and in unbearable pain. If you will just remember her nature, her ways, and her true worth, you will recognize that in her you never possessed nor lost anything that was beautiful. I don't think I'll have to work very hard to get you to remember this.

"Whenever she came before you in the past and spoke sweetly, you always used to attack her and drive her away with courageous words drawn from

subita mutatio rerum non sine quodam quasi fluctu contingit animorum; sic factum est ut tu quoque paulisper a tua tranquillitate descisceres. Sed tempus est haurire te aliquid ac degustare molle atque iucundum quod ad interiora transmissum validioribus haustibus viam fecerit. Adsit igitur rhetoricae suadela dulcedinis quae tum tantum recto calle procedit, cum nostra instituta non deserit cumque hac Musica laris nostri vernacula nunc leviores nunc graviores modos succinat.

"Quid est igitur, o homo, quod te in maestitiam luctumque deiecit? Novum, credo, aliquid inusitatumque vidisti. Tu fortunam putas erga te esse mutatam; erras. Hi semper eius mores sunt ista natura. Servavit circa te propriam potius in ipsa sui mutabilitate constantiam. Talis erat cum blandiebatur, cum tibi falsae inlecebris felicitatis alluderet. Deprehendisti caeci numinis ambiguos vultus. Quae sese adhuc velat aliis, tota tibi prorsus innotuit. Si probas, utere moribus; ne queraris. Si perfidiam perhorrescis, sperne atque abice perniciosa ludentem. Nam quae nunc tibi est tanti causa maeroris, haec eadem tranquillitatis esse debuisset. Reliquit enim te quam non relicturam nemo umquam poterit esse securus.

my innermost shrine.[2] But in truth, every sudden change in circumstances happens with its own kind of flood against the soul. Thus it happened to you, so that for a little while you abandoned your peace of mind. But it is now time for you to drink down and taste some medicine gentle and pleasant, which once you have absorbed will prepare the way for stronger remedies. So now let me apply the persuasion of sweet rhetoric—which only travels the right path when it follows my instructions—and with it, let music from my own halls sing in harmony, first in lighter and then in more solemn tones.

"What is it then, mortal man, that has cast you down into such sorrow and grief? I do believe you have seen something new and strange to you. You think that Fortune has changed regarding you—but you're wrong. These have always been her ways and nature. She indeed has remained constant toward you in her very changeability. She was just the same when she was flattering you and tricking you with promises of false happiness. You have now seen the changing face of that blind goddess.[3] She who still hides herself from others has completely revealed herself to you. If you are content with her, make use of her ways and don't complain. If you're horrified by her treachery, reject her and flee from someone playing such a wicked game. This one who now is such a cause of sorrow to you should have brought

"An vero tu pretiosam aestimas abituram felicitatem? Et cara tibi est fortuna praesens nec manendi fida et cum discesserit adlatura maerorem? Quod si nec ex arbitrio retineri potest et calamitosos fugiens facit, quid est aliud fugax quam futurae quoddam calamitatis indicium? Neque enim quod ante oculos situm est, suffecerit intueri; rerum exitus prudentia metitur eademque in alterutro mutabilitas nec formidandas fortunae minas nec exoptandas facit esse blanditias. Postremo aequo animo toleres oportet quidquid intra fortunae aream geritur, cum semel iugo eius colla submiseris. Quod si manendi abeundique scribere legem velis ei quam tu tibi dominam sponte legisti, nonne iniurius fueris et inpatientia sortem exacerbes quam permutare non possis? Si ventis vela committeres, non quo voluntas peteret sed quo flatus impellerent, promoveres; si arvis semina crederes, feraces inter se annos sterilesque pensares. Fortunae te regendum dedisti; dominae moribus oportet obtemperes. Tu vero volventis rotae impetum retinere conaris? At, omnium mortalium stolidissime, si manere incipit, fors esse desistit.

you peace of mind.[4] She who abandoned you will never be a source of security to anyone.

"Do you really value the kind of happiness that will pass away? Is present Fortune dear to you if she can't be trusted to stay and if she brings such sorrow when she leaves? But if she can't be retained by your will and she makes people miserable when she flees, what is she except a sign of approaching calamity? It is not enough to simply look at what is placed before our eyes at this moment. Prudence demands that we also consider the end of things. The ability of Fortune to move in either direction means we should neither fear her threats nor hope for her favors. Finally you have to calmly endure whatever happens on her own ground once you submit your neck to Fortune's yoke. If you try to impose your rules on her coming and going once you've willingly given her authority over your life, won't your impatience make worse the circumstances you're not able to change? If you spread your sails to the wind, you must go wherever the weather blows you, not the direction you want to go. If you entrust your seeds to the field, you have to accept the good years with the bad. Since you've given yourself to the rule of Fortune, you have to submit yourself to her ways. Would you try to hold back her wheel from turning?[5] O most foolish of men! If Fortune became constant, she would no longer be herself.

"Vellem autem pauca tecum fortunae ipsius verbis agitare. Tu igitur an ius postulet, animadverte.

"'Quid tu homo ream me cotidianis agis querelis? Quam tibi fecimus iniuriam? Quae tua tibi detraximus bona? Quovis iudice de opum dignitatumque mecum possessione contende. Et si cuiusquam mortalium proprium quid horum esse monstraveris, ego iam tua fuisse quae repetis, sponte concedam.

"'Cum te matris utero natura produxit, nudum rebus omnibus inopemque suscepi, meis opibus fovi, et quod te nunc inpatientem nostri facit, favore prona indulgentius educavi, omnium quae mei iuris sunt affluentia et splendore circumdedi. Nunc mihi retrahere manum libet. Habes gratiam velut usus alienis, non habes ius querelae tamquam prorsus tua perdideris. Quid igitur ingemiscis? Nulla tibi a nobis est allata violentia. Opes honores ceteraque talium mei sunt iuris. Dominam famulae cognoscunt; mecum veniunt, me abeunte discedunt. Audacter adfirmem, si tua forent quae amissa conquereris nullo modo perdidisses.

Fortune Speaks

"I would like to say a few things to you now in the voice of Fortune herself. You judge whether or not you think her words are fair:

"'O mortal man, why do you put me on trial every day with your complaints? What injury have I done you? What goods of yours have I stolen away? Accuse me before any judge you like concerning riches and honors. If you can demonstrate that any of these things properly belong to any mortal, then I will freely concede that the things you seek are yours.

"'When nature brought you forth from your mother's womb, naked and lacking in everything, I took you in my arms. I pampered you with my wealth and—this is what makes you so impatient with me now—I raised you quite indulgently with my kind favor and surrounded you with all the abundance and splendor that was in my power. Now it pleases me to draw back my hand. You should thank me as someone who borrowed the goods of another and not be complaining that you have lost something that was never yours. So why are you moaning? I have done no violence to you. Riches, honors, and other such things are all mine by right. These slaves know their mistress. They come with me and leave when I leave. So let me tell

"'An ego sola meum ius exercere prohibebor? Licet caelo proferre lucidos dies eosdemque tenebrosis noctibus condere. Licet anno terrae vultum nunc floribus frugibusque redimire, nunc nimbis frigoribusque confundere. Ius est mari nunc strato aequore blandiri, nunc procellis ac fluctibus inhorrescere. Nos ad constantiam nostris moribus alienam inexpleta hominum cupiditas alligabit? Haec nostra vis est, hunc continuum ludum ludimus; rotam volubili orbe versamus, infima summis summa infimis mutare gaudemus. Ascende si placet, sed ea lege ne utique cum ludicri mei ratio poscet, descendere iniuriam putes.

"'An tu mores ignorabas meos? Nesciebas Croesum regem Lydorum Cyro paulo ante formidabilem mox deinde miserandum rogi flammis traditum misso caelitus imbre defensum? Num te praeterit Paulum Persi regis a se capti calamitatibus pias inpendisse lacrimas? Quid tragoediarum clamor aliud deflet nisi indiscreto ictu fortunam felicia regna vertentem? Nonne adulescentulus δοιοὺς πίθους τὸν μὲν ἕνα κακῶν τὸν δ' ἕτερον ἐάων in Iovis limine iacere didicisti?

you with all confidence that if those things you are complaining about had ever truly been yours, you would not have lost them in the first place.

"'Am I alone prohibited from exercising my rights? The heavens are allowed to bring forth brilliant days and then hide them in the shadows of night. The seasons are permitted to crown the face of the earth with flowers and fruit, then darken it with cloud and cold. The sea is allowed to entice with calm waters, then quickly stir up storms and swell. Will insatiable human greed then bind me to a constancy alien to my ways? This is my strength, this is my endless game. I spin my wheel in a swift and ever-turning circle. I rejoice to bring the bottom to the top and the top to the bottom. Climb up high if you wish, but on this condition—don't think yourself wronged when the rules of my game send you back down again.

"'Did you truly not know my ways? Didn't you know about Croesus, the king of the Lydians? Just a short time earlier he was the formidable enemy of Cyrus, then in an instant became a man to be pitied as he was handed over to be burned at the stake, then saved suddenly by a rain shower.[6] Surely you at least remember that Paullus wept honorable tears for the disasters that befell his captive Perseus.[7] What is it that tragic drama bewails if not Fortune with her indiscriminate blows overturning happy

"'Quid si uberius de bonorum parte sumpsisti? Quid si a te non tota discessi? Quid si haec ipsa mei mutabilitas iusta tibi causa est sperandi meliora? Tamen ne animo contabescas et intra commune omnibus regnum locatus proprio vivere iure desideres.'"

"His igitur si pro se tecum fortuna loqueretur, quid profecto contra hisceres non haberes, aut si quid est quo querelam tuam iure tuearis, proferas oportet. Dabimus dicendi locum."

Tum ego: "Speciosa quidem ista sunt," inquam, "oblitaque Rhetoricae ac Musicae melle dulcedinis; tum tantum, cum audiuntur, oblectant. Sed miseris malorum altior sensus est. Itaque cum haec auribus insonare desierint, insitus animum maeror praegravat."

Et illa: "Ita est," inquit. "Haec enim nondum morbi tui remedia sed adhuc contumacis adversum

kingdoms? Didn't you learn as a child that Jupiter has on his threshold two jars, one full of evil and the other full of good?[8]

"'What if you've drawn too deeply from the jar holding good? What if I haven't completely deserted you? What if this very mutability of mine should be a source of hope for better things to you? Even so, you shouldn't waste away in your own heart desiring to live by your own private law, for you reside in a kingdom that embraces all people.'"

Count Your Blessings

"If Fortune were to speak with you in this way to defend herself, you wouldn't have anything to say in response, would you? But if you do have a defense for your complaints, then out with it now. I will give you the opportunity to speak."

So I spoke: "These arguments of yours sound very pretty—smeared as they are with the honey of rhetoric and poetry—but only while they are being heard. For those of us who are actually suffering, the pain goes much too deep. As soon as your words stop ringing in my ears, the grief in my heart weighs me down again."

"That's fair enough," she said. "My words were not meant as a cure for your illness, but only as a

curationem doloris fomenta quaedam sunt. Nam quae in profundum sese penetrent, cum tempestivum fuerit admovebo.

"Verumtamen ne te existimari miserum velis, an numerum modumque tuae felicitatis oblitus es? Taceo quod desolatum parente summorum te virorum cura suscepit delectusque in affinitatem principum civitatis, quod pretiosissimum propinquitatis genus est, prius carus quam proximus esse coepisti. Quis non te felicissimum cum tanto splendore socerorum, cum coniugis pudore, cum masculae quoque prolis opportunitate praedicavit? Praetereo, libet enim praeterire communia, sumptas in adulescentia negatas senibus dignitates; ad singularem felicitatis tuae cumulum venire delectat.

"Si quis rerum mortalium fructus ullum beatitudinis pondus habet, poteritne illius memoria lucis quantalibet ingruentium malorum mole deleri, cum duos pariter consules liberos tuos domo provehi sub frequentia patrum, sub plebis alacritate vidisti, cum eisdem in curia curules insidentibus tu regiae

temporary balm for your pain that has so stubbornly resisted a remedy until now. When the time is right, I'll apply medicines that will penetrate deep within your soul.

"In the meantime would you please stop thinking of yourself as a miserable wretch! Have you forgotten how much happiness and what sorts of kindness you've enjoyed in your life? I won't even mention how the very best people took you into their care when your father died and how you were welcomed into the homes of the leading citizens of the state.[9] Even before you were made a part of their family you became dear to them, the most valuable kind of kinship there is. Who didn't call you the happiest of men because of the splendor of your in-laws, the modesty of your wife, and the blessings of your sons after you? I will pass over—since it would be immodest to bring up what is common knowledge—the great honors given you in your youth, honors denied to older men. I would rather move on to that one thing that brought you your greatest happiness.

"If anything in this mortal world has brought any measure of joy, wouldn't it be that day—and no memory of that most glorious time will ever be destroyed by any invading evils however great—when you saw your two sons carried forth together from your home as consuls by a throng of senators to

laudis orator ingenii gloriam facundiaeque meruisti, cum in circo duorum medius consulum circumfusae multitudinis expectationem triumphali largitione satiasti?

"Dedisti ut opinor verba fortunae, dum te illa demulcet, dum te ut delicias suas fovet. Munus quod nulli umquam privato commodaverat abstulisti. Visne igitur cum fortuna calculum ponere? Nunc te primum liventi oculo praestrinxit. Si numerum modumque laetorum tristiumve consideres, adhuc te felicem negare non possis. Quod si idcirco te fortunatum esse non aestimas, quoniam quae tunc laeta videbantur abierunt, non est quod te miserum putes, quoniam quae nunc creduntur maesta praetereunt.

"An tu in hanc vitae scaenam nunc primum subitus hospesque venisti? Ullamne humanis rebus inesse constantiam reris, cum ipsum saepe hominem velox hora dissolvat? Nam etsi rara est fortuitis manendi fides, ultimus tamen vitae dies mors

the acclaim of the common people?[10] While they both sat in the consular chairs in the Senate chamber, didn't you deliver your oration in praise of the king and earn the glory heaped on you for your famed eloquence? Then at the Circus Maximus, with your sons as consuls on each side, didn't you satisfy the expectations of the crowds all around you with the distribution of generous gifts worthy of a triumphant general?[11]

"I think you beguiled Fortune while she was caressing you and favoring you as her darling. You stole from her a gift that she had never before bestowed on a private citizen. Do you then really want to see her balance sheet?[12] Now, for the first time, she has looked on you with a jealous eye. If you were to consider the number and measure of your joys and sorrows, you couldn't deny that up to this point in your life you have been happy. So even if you don't consider yourself fortunate here in current circumstances because the blessings that once brought you happiness have disappeared, please don't think yourself miserable since the calamities that now bring you sorrow will also pass away.

"Have you suddenly walked onto the stage of life as if a visitor for the first time? Do you think there is any constancy in human affairs, when one swift hour often turns a person into nothing? Even if, as rarely happens, the gifts of Fortune remain steady,

quaedam fortunae est etiam manentis. Quid igitur referre putas, tune illam moriendo deseras an te illa fugiendo?"

Tum ego: "Vera," inquam, "commemoras, O virtutum omnium nutrix, nec infitiari possum prosperitatis meae velocissimum cursum. Sed hoc est quod recolentem vehementius coquit. Nam in omni adversitate fortunae infelicissimum est genus infortunii fuisse felicem."

"Sed quod tu," inquit, "falsae opinionis supplicium luas, id rebus iure imputare non possis. Nam si te hoc inane nomen fortuitae felicitatis movet, quam pluribus maximisque abundes mecum reputes licet. Igitur si quod in omni fortunae tuae censu pretiosissimum possidebas, id tibi divinitus inlaesum adhuc inviolatumque servatur, poterisne meliora quaeque retinens de infortunio iure causari?

"Atqui viget incolumis illud pretiosissimum generis humani decus Symmachus socer et quod vitae pretio non segnis emeres, vir totus ex sapientia

the last day of life itself will be a kind of death for Fortune if she has lingered. What difference do you think it makes then whether you desert Fortune by dying or she deserts you by fleeing away?"

What Is Happiness?

Then I said, "O nourisher of all virtues, what you remind me of is true. I can't deny that the course of my success was amazingly swift. That's the reason it burns so painfully to remember it. Of the misfortunes in life, the most bitter is to have once been happy."[13]

"But," she said, "you must realize that you're suffering this punishment because of your false beliefs. You cannot justly blame anything else for that. If you are moved by this empty idea that Fortune brings happiness, consider with me how many and how great are your blessings still. If you even now possess the most precious gifts that Fortune gave you and if they are protected still, safe and unharmed, by divine influence, will you be able to complain about misfortune while you continue to hold on to these better things?

"Consider that your father-in-law Symmachus, that most precious ornament of the human race, is alive and thriving.[14] He has no care for himself but

virtutibusque factus suarum securus tuis ingemiscit iniuriis. Vivit uxor ingenio modesta, pudicitia pudore praecellenset, ut omnes eius dotes breviter includam, patri similis. Vivit inquam tibique tantum vitae huius exosa spiritum servat quoque uno felicitatem minui tuam vel ipsa concesserim, tui desiderio lacrimis ac dolore tabescit. Quid dicam liberos consulares quorum iam, ut in id aetatis pueris, vel paterni vel aviti specimen elucet ingenii?

"Cum igitur praecipua sit mortalibus vitae cura retinendae, o te si tua bona cognoscas felicem, cui suppetunt etiam nunc quae vita nemo dubitat esse cariora! Quare sicca iam lacrimas. Nondum est ad unum omnes exosa fortuna nec tibi nimium valida tempestas incubuit, quando tenaces haerent ancorae quae nec praesentis solamen nec futuri spem temporis abesse patiantur."

"Et haereant," inquam, "precor; illis namque manentibus, utcumque se res habeant, enatabimus. Sed quantum ornamentis nostris decesserit, vides."

groans ceaselessly for your afflictions. He is a man completely shaped by wisdom and virtue—such gifts as you would eagerly purchase at the cost of your life. Your wife still lives, a woman modest by nature, excelling all in chastity and honor. In a word, she is in all her gifts like her father.[15] When I say she lives, I mean she draws breath for you alone but otherwise despises this life. In this one thing I will admit that your life is indeed worse than it once was: She wastes away with tears and longing for you. And finally what can I say about your two sons the consuls, who even in their youth now shine forth in the likeness of their father and grandfather?[16]

"Although it is the particular nature of mortals to try to preserve their lives, how happy you would be if you only realized the good things you truly possess. Even now you have those treasures that no one would doubt are dearer than life itself. So please dry your tears. Fortune does not yet hate all your blessings nor is the storm which strikes you so fierce that you have lost what is holding you firm, those anchors that will not allow you to lose your consolation in the present nor your hope for the future."

"And I pray they may indeed hold firm," I said. "If they do, I might be able to swim out of this flood no matter what happens. But you can plainly see how many of my honors I have lost!"

Et illa: "Promovimus," inquit, "aliquantum, si te nondum totius tuae sortis piget. Sed delicias tuas ferre non possum qui abesse aliquid tuae beatitudini tam luctuosus atque anxius conqueraris. Quis est enim tam conpositae felicitatis ut non aliqua ex parte cum status sui qualitate rixetur? Anxia enim res est humanorum condicio bonorum et quae vel numquam tota proveniat vel numquam perpetua subsistat. Huic census exuberat, sed est pudori degener sanguis; hunc nobilitas notum facit, sed angustia rei familiaris inclusus esse mallet ignotus. Ille utroque circumfluus vitam caelibem deflet; ille nuptiis felix orbus liberis alieno censum nutrit heredi. Alius prole laetatus filii filiaeve delictis maestus inlacrimat. Idcirco nemo facile cum fortunae suae condicione concordat; inest enim singulis quod inexpertus ignoret, expertus exhorreat.

"Adde quod felicissimi cuiusque delicatissimus sensus est et nisi ad nutum cuncta suppetant, omnis adversitatis insolens minimis quibusque prosternitur; adeo perexigua sunt quae fortunatissimis beatitudinis summam detrahunt. Quam multos esse coniectas qui sese caelo proximos arbitrentur, si de

"At least we've moved forward a little bit," she sighed, "if you're no longer completely in despair about your lot in your life. But what I can't stand is your childish self-pity and whining that something is missing from your happiness. I mean, who has ever had a life so joyful that they couldn't complain about some problem? Anxiety is part of the human condition. The good things in life are never good enough, nor do they last forever. One man rejoices in his wealth but is ashamed of his humble birth. Another man has famous ancestors but is so ashamed of his poverty that he prefers to remain unknown. Yet another man has both wealth and noble birth but is unhappy because he has no wife. Still another is happily married but has no children, so he builds his estate for a stranger to inherit. Then another rejoices that he has children but bemoans the failings of his son or daughter. This is why no one is happy with the state of their fortune in life. There is for each of us some problem that means little to those who haven't experienced it but terrifies those who have.

"Consider also that the happiest people are also the most sensitive to misfortune, so that unless everything goes exactly according to their wishes, they are easily thrown into despair because they have the least experience with adversity. Those things of the least importance are the ones that drag the

fortunae tuae reliquiis pars eis minima contingat? Hic ipse locus quem tu exilium vocas, incolentibus patria est.

"Adeo nihil est miserum nisi cum putes contraque beata sors omnis est aequanimitate tolerantis. Quis est ille tam felix qui cum dederit inpatientiae manus, statum suum mutare non optet? Quam multis amaritudinibus humanae felicitatis dulcedo respersa est! Quae si etiam fruenti iucunda esse videatur, tamen quo minus cum velit abeat retineri non possit. Liquet igitur quam sit mortalium rerum misera beatitudo quae nec apud aequanimos perpetua perdurat nec anxios tota delectat.

"Quid igitur, o mortales, extra petitis intra vos positam felicitatem? Error vos inscitiaque confundit. Ostendam breviter tibi summae cardinem felicitatis.

"Estne aliquid tibi te ipso pretiosius? 'Nihil,' inquies. Igitur si tui compos fueris, possidebis quod nec tu amittere umquam velis nec fortuna possit auferre. Atque ut agnoscas in his fortuitis rebus beatitudinem constare non posse, sic collige. Si beatitudo

most fortunate people down from the height of their happiness. Do you know how many people there are who would believe themselves practically in the heavens if they had only the smallest part of what you have? This condition of yours you call unbearable exile is home to those who live there.

"No situation is hopelessly miserable unless you think it is. Likewise every lot in life is blessed if you bear it with contentment. Who is so happy that when he gives in to impatience he wouldn't want to change his condition? How much bitterness is sprinkled on the sweetness of human joy! And although this sweetness seems pleasant to whoever is enjoying it, it can't be prevented from disappearing whenever it wishes. Therefore it's clear how lacking this happiness in human affairs really is, since it neither endures for those who are content nor completely satisfies the troubled.

"O mortals, why do you look outside yourselves for the happiness that is within you? Error and ignorance overwhelm you. And so I will in a few words reveal to you, Boethius, the source of the highest happiness.

"Is there anything more precious to you than yourself? 'Nothing,' you will answer. Therefore, if you have mastery over yourself, you will possess something you would never want to lose and that Fortune cannot take away from you. And so

est summum naturae bonum ratione degentis nec est summum bonum quod eripi ullo modo potest, quoniam praecellit id quod nequeat auferri, manifestum est quoniam ad beatitudinem percipiendam fortunae instabilitas adspirare non possit.

"Ad haec quem caduca ista felicitas vehit vel scit eam vel nescit esse mutabilem. Si nescit, quaenam beata sors esse potest ignorantiae caecitate? Si scit, metuat necesse est, ne amittat quod amitti posse non dubitat; quare continuus timor non sinit esse felicem. An vel si amiserit, neglegendum putat? Sic quoque perexile bonum est quod aequo animo feratur amissum.

"Et quoniam tu idem es cui persuasum atque insitum permultis demonstrationibus scio mentes hominum nullo modo esse mortales cumque clarum sit fortuitam felicitatem corporis morte finiri, dubitari nequit, si haec afferre beatitudinem potest, quin omne mortalium genus in miseriam mortis fine labatur. Quod si multos scimus beatitudinis fructum non morte solum verum etiam doloribus suppliciisque quaesisse, quonam modo praesens facere beatos potest quae miseros transacta non efficit?

that you might recognize that genuine happiness does not consist of the things that Fortune brings you, consider this. If happiness is the highest good for a rational human being and if the highest good is something that cannot be stolen away by any means—given that what is best cannot be taken—then it is obvious that the instability of Fortune cannot hope to bring about true happiness.

"Consider as well that whoever is carried along by this kind of fallible happiness either knows or doesn't know that it will not last. If he doesn't know, what kind of happiness can someone who lives a life of blind ignorance have? If he does know, then he must fear that he will lose that which he knows will be lost, and thus constant fear doesn't allow him to be happy. Or maybe he thinks it doesn't matter if he does lose it. In that case, it can't have been a lasting good if he can bear so easily to lose it.

"And since I know that you are a man who has been persuaded by many sound arguments that the human soul is in no way mortal and since it is also clear that any happiness brought by Fortune ends with the death of the body, then it cannot be doubted that if Fortune is able to bring about happiness, the whole human race is sliding toward misery at their end, which is death. But since we know that many have sought the reward of happiness not only through death but also by sorrow and suffering,[17]

"Sed quoniam rationum iam in te mearum fomenta descendunt, paulo validioribus utendum puto. Age enim si iam caduca et momentaria fortunae dona non essent, quid in eis est quod aut vestrum umquam fieri queat aut non perspectum consideratumque vilescat?

"Divitiaene vel vestrae vel sui natura pretiosae sunt? Quid earum potius, aurumne an vis congesta pecuniae? Atqui haec effundendo magis quam coacervando melius nitent, si quidem avaritia semper odiosos, claros largitas facit. Quod si manere apud quemque non potest quod transfertur in alterum, tunc est pretiosa pecunia cum translata in alios largiendi usu desinit possideri. At eadem si apud unum quanta est ubique gentium congeratur, ceteros sui inopes fecerit. Et vox quidem tota pariter multorum replet auditum; vestrae vero divitiae nisi comminutae in plures transire non possunt. Quod cum factum est, pauperes necesse est faciant quos relinquunt. O igitur angustas inopesque divitias

then how can the happiness brought by Fortune in this life make people truly happy when its passing away in death does not make them miserable?

Wealth

"But since the medicines of my arguments are now working their way into you, I think it's time to use something stronger. Come now, even if the gifts of Fortune were not fleeting and momentary, what would you ever find in them that could be truly yours and wouldn't seem worthless on close examination and careful consideration?

"Are riches valuable because they belong to you or because of their own nature? What kind of wealth is most valuable? Gold perhaps or the power of hoarded riches? But these shine more brightly by being poured out rather than by being heaped up, for greed makes people hated, while generosity makes them popular. And since that which is given to another is not able to stay with someone, then money is only valuable when it is given away and is no longer possessed. If all the money in the world were to be gathered together in the possession of one person, no one else would have any. A sound equally fills the ears of everyone who hears it, but money isn't able to pass to others unless it

quas nec habere totas pluribus licet et ad quemlibet sine ceterorum paupertate non veniunt!

"An gemmarum fulgor oculos trahit? Sed si quid est in hoc splendore praecipui, gemmarum est lux illa non hominum, quas quidem mirari homines vehementer admiror. Quid est enim carens animae motu atque compage quod animatae rationabilique naturae pulchrum esse iure videatur? Quae tametsi conditoris opera suique distinctione postremae aliquid pulchritudinis trahunt, infra vestram tamen excellentiam conlocatae admirationem vestram nullo modo merebantur.

"An vos agrorum pulchritudo delectat? Quidni? Est enim pulcherrimi operis pulchra portio. Sic quondam sereni maris facie gaudemus; sic caelum sidera lunam solemque miramur. Num te horum aliquid attingit? Num audes alicuius talium splendore gloriari? An vernis floribus ipse distingueris aut tua in aestivos fructus intumescit ubertas? Quid inanibus gaudiis raperis? Quid externa bona pro tuis amplexaris? Numquam tua faciet esse fortuna quae a te natura rerum fecit aliena. Terrarum quidem fructus animantium procul dubio debentur alimentis. Sed si, quod naturae satis est, replere indigentiam

is divided. However, when this happens those who lose their wealth by necessity become poor. O how limited and impoverished riches are! They can't be shared by everyone equally and they can't come to any one person without making everyone else poor.

"Perhaps the splendor of jewels attracts your eyes? But if there is anything excellent in their radiance, that light belongs to the jewels, not to you. Therefore I am utterly amazed how humans marvel at them. What is there that lacks the movement and structure of a soul that can rightly seem beautiful to a being having a rational nature? Even if by the work of their creator and by their own distinct qualities such things reflect some smallest measure of lasting beauty, they remain far below your own excellence and are not at all worthy of your admiration.

"Do you delight in the beauty of countryside? And why shouldn't you? It is a beautiful part of a most glorious creation. In a similar way, we sometimes delight in the tranquil face of the sea or marvel at the heavens, stars, moon, and sun. But do any of these things belong to you? Would you dare to boast in the splendor of any of them? Do *you* shine forth in flowering glory in the springtime? Do *you* swell abundantly with summer fruit? Why then are you captivated by empty splendors? Why do you embrace external goods as if they were your own? Fortune will never make things yours that nature

velis, nihil est quod fortunae affluentiam petas. Paucis enim minimisque natura contenta est, cuius satietatem si superfluis urgere velis, aut iniucundum quod infuderis fiet aut noxium.

"Iam vero pulchrum variis fulgere vestibus putas, quarum si grata intuitu species est, aut materiae naturam aut ingenium mirabor artificis. An vero te longus ordo famulorum facit esse felicem? Qui si vitiosi moribus sint, perniciosa domus sarcina et ipsi domino vehementer inimica; sin vero probi, quonam modo in tuis opibus aliena probitas numerabitur? Ex quibus omnibus nihil horum quae tu in tuis conputas bonis tuum esse bonum liquido monstratur. Quibus si nihil inest appetendae pulchritudinis, quid est quod vel amissis doleas vel laeteris retentis? Quod si natura pulchra sunt, quid id tua refert? Nam haec per se a tuis quoque opibus sequestrata placuissent. Neque enim idcirco sunt pretiosa quod in tuas venere divitias, sed quoniam pretiosa videbantur, tuis ea divitiis adnumerare maluisti.

has made to be outside you. Of course the fruits of the earth were made to nourish living beings. But if you limit your desires to satisfying your needs—which is what nature intends—there's no reason to seek an excess from Fortune. Nature is content with just a few, small things. If you wish to overwhelm what is sufficient for her with overabundance, what you pile on top will become unpleasant or even harmful to you.

"Now perhaps you think it's a beautiful thing to look splendid in all kinds of clothing? But if clothing is pleasing to look at, then it's the nature of the material or the skill of the tailor that you should admire. Or perhaps you're pleased by a long line of slaves[18] following you about? But consider that if they're corrupt in their ways then they will be a ruinous burden on your household and dangerous to you as a master. On the other hand, if they are honest and upright, how can the virtue of someone else be numbered among your own strengths? From all this it's clear that nothing you reckon among your goods is truly in your possession. So if there's no beauty to be sought in them, why do you grieve if you lose them or rejoice if you keep them? But if they're beautiful by their own nature, how is that a credit to you? They would still be pleasing to you even if they weren't part of your property. They're not valuable because they were

"Quid autem tanto fortunae strepitu desideratis? Fugare credo indigentiam copia quaeritis. Atqui hoc vobis in contrarium cedit. Pluribus quippe adminiculis opus est ad tuendam pretiosae supellectilis varietatem, verumque illud est permultis eos indigere qui permulta possideant contraque minimum qui abundantiam suam naturae necessitate non ambitus superfluitate metiantur.

"Itane autem nullum est proprium vobis atque insitum bonum ut in externis ac sepositis rebus bona vestra quaeratis? Sic rerum versa condicio est ut divinum merito rationis animal non aliter sibi splendere nisi inanimatae supellectilis possessione videatur? Et alia quidem suis contenta sunt; vos autem deo mente consimiles ab rebus infimis excellentis naturae ornamenta captatis nec intellegitis quantum conditori vestro faciatis iniuriam. Ille genus humanum terrenis omnibus praestare voluit; vos dignitatem vestram infra infima quaeque detruditis.

"Nam si omne cuiusque bonum eo cuius est constat esse pretiosius, cum vilissima rerum vestra bona

added to your riches. No, it is because they seemed precious that you wanted to include them among your possessions.

"What is it that all you mortals are seeking from Fortune as you cry out so loudly against her? I think you're trying to flee your own insatiable desires by always seeking more. But this never works for you—just the opposite! You end up needing ever more resources to preserve your many precious treasures. In truth those who have much need much. On the other hand, those who measure their wealth not by greed but only by what nature requires need very little.

"Are there really no innate goods within you so that you have to seek out possessions in external and separate things? Are matters so upside down with you mortals that you—animals made divine by virtue of reason—never seem splendid to yourselves except when you possess inanimate objects? All other creatures are content with their own, but you, though you are like God in having minds, seek to adorn your superior nature with inferior things. Don't you realize the injury you do to your creator? For God wanted the human race to stand above all earthly creatures, but you have trampled your honor beneath the lowest of things.

"For if it is agreed that the good of something is more valuable than the one to whom it belongs, then

esse iudicatis, eisdem vosmet ipsos vestra existimatione submittitis, quod quidem haud immerito cadit. Humanae quippe naturae ista condicio est ut tum tantum ceteris rebus cum se cognoscit excellat, eadem tamen infra bestias redigatur, si se nosse desierit. Nam ceteris animantibus sese ignorare naturae est; hominibus vitio venit.

"Quam vero late patet vester hic error qui ornari posse aliquid ornamentis existimatis alienis? At id fieri nequit. Nam si quid ex appositis luceat, ipsa quidem quae sunt apposita laudantur; illud vero his tectum atque velatum in sua nihilo minus foeditate perdurat.

"Ego vero nego ullum esse bonum quod noceat habenti. Num id mentior? 'Minime,' inquis. Atqui divitiae possidentibus persaepe nocuerunt, cum pessimus quisque eoque alieni magis avidus quidquid usquam auri gemmarumque est se solum qui habeat dignissimum putat. Tu igitur qui nunc contum gladiumque sollicitus pertimescis, si vitae huius callem vacuus viator intrasses, coram latrone cantares. O praeclara opum mortalium beatitudo quam cum adeptus fueris securus esse desistis!

you mortals judge the lowest of things to be more valuable than yourselves when you make them your possessions—and that seems to me a fair judgment. Indeed the condition of human nature is such that it only surpasses all other things when it knows itself.[19] But that same nature is reduced to being lower than the beasts if it stops knowing itself. It is the nature of animals not to be aware of themselves, but for humans it is a grave fault.

"How far you have wandered from the truth when you think that something can be improved by external ornaments! This simply cannot be. For if any radiance shines forth from what has been attached to something, it is the attachments themselves that are praised. That which is covered and hidden by them remains as ugly as ever.

"Now," she said, "I maintain that nothing is good which harms the one possessing it. Am I lying? 'Not at all,' you will say. But riches have very often harmed the one possessing them, for the worst sort of people are greedy to seize whatever gold and gems they don't own because they think that they alone are most worthy of them. But you, who now are so terrified of the spear and the sword, would sing as you passed by a robber if you had set out on the road of this life an empty-handed traveler.[20] O how wonderful the blessing of mortal riches! Once you gain them, you will never be safe again.

"Quid autem de dignitatibus potentiaque disseram quae vos verae dignitatis ac potestatis inscii caelo exaequatis? Quae si in improbissimum quemque ceciderunt, quae flammis Aetnae eructantibus, quod diluvium tantas strages dederint? Certe, uti meminisse te arbitror, consulare imperium, quod libertatis principium fuerat, ob superbiam consulum vestri veteres abolere cupiverunt, qui ob eandem superbiam prius regium de civitate nomen abstulerant. At si quando, quod perrarum est, probis deferantur, quid in eis aliud quam probitas utentium placet? Ita fit ut non virtutibus ex dignitate sed ex virtute dignitatibus honor accedat.

"Quae vero est ista vestra expetibilis ac praeclara potentia? Nonne, o terrena animalia, consideratis quibus qui praesidere videamini? Nunc si inter mures videres unum aliquem ius sibi ac potestatem prae ceteris vindicantem, quanto movereris cachinno! Quid vero, si corpus spectes, inbecillius homine reperire queas quos saepe muscularum quoque vel morsus vel in secreta quaeque reptantium necat introitus? Quo vero quisquam ius aliquod in quempiam nisi in solum corpus et quod infra corpus

Honor and Power

"What should I say then about positions of honor and power? You praise these things to the heavens, being ignorant of what true honor and real power are. When such things have fallen into the hands of the most wicked men, what volcanoes[21] with torrents of flame or raging floods have caused greater destruction? I'm certain you'll remember that your ancestors wanted to abolish the power of the consuls, the foundation of liberty, because of consular arrogance, just as earlier they had erased the very name of king from the state because of royal pride.[22] But when power is handed over to righteous people (a rare occurrence indeed), what do we praise them for but the just use of that power? So it isn't the office you hold that brings honor to your virtues, but your innate virtues that bring honor to the office.

"Truly what is this so-called power of yours that is so desirable, so glorious? O earthly creatures, do you ever consider who it is you think you command? Now if you, Boethius, ever saw a tiny mouse claiming to exercise power and authority over his fellow mice, wouldn't you laugh? But if you were to consider the body, what could you find weaker than human beings, who often are killed by a little fly that bites or creeps its way deep inside the flesh? How can someone exert power over anyone else

est, fortunam loquor, possit exserere? Num quidquam libero imperabis animo? Num mentem firma sibi ratione cohaerentem de statu propriae quietis amovebis? Cum liberum quendam virum suppliciis se tyrannus adacturum putaret, ut adversum se factae coniurationis conscios proderet, linguam ille momordit atque abscidit et in os tyranni saevientis abiecit; ita cruciatus, quos putabat tyrannus materiam crudelitatis, vir sapiens fecit esse virtutis.

"Quid autem est quod in alium facere quisquam possit, quod sustinere ab alio ipse non possit? Busiridem accipimus necare hospites solitum ab Hercule hospite fuisse mactatum. Regulus plures Poenorum bello captos in vincla coniecerat, sed mox ipse victorum catenis manus praebuit. Ullamne igitur eius hominis potentiam putas, qui quod ipse in alio potest, ne id in se alter valeat efficere non possit?

"Ad haec si ipsis dignitatibus ac potestatibus inesset aliquid naturalis ac proprii boni, numquam pessimis provenirent. Neque enim sibi solent adversa sociari; natura respuit ut contraria quaeque iungantur. Ita cum pessimos plerumque dignitatibus fungi dubium non sit, illud etiam liquet natura sui bona non esse quae se pessimis haerere patiantur. Quod quidem

except over their body and that which is lower than the body, by which I mean their fortune? Surely you cannot command a spirit that is free. Surely you cannot move the mind of someone who is fixed by firm reason from their proper place of quiet calm. Once there was a tyrant who thought he could compel by torture a certain free man to betray those conspiring with him, but that man instead bit his tongue in half and ripped it out, throwing it into the face of the angry ruler. So the tortures the tyrant thought would be an opportunity for cruelties, the wise man made an occasion for virtue.[23]

"Indeed is there anything you can do to another person that another person cannot do to you? We've all heard the story of Busiris, who used to slaughter his guests until Hercules killed him.[24] Regulus put many Carthaginian war prisoners in chains, but soon enough held out his own hands for the chains of his captors.[25] Do you think then that a man has any real power if he is unable to prevent someone from doing to him what he can do to others?

"Consider as well that if there were any natural and inherent good in offices and powers themselves, they would never come into the possession of those who are most evil. For opposites do not usually join themselves together, since nature revolts against the combination of contrary things. Therefore, since there's no doubt that the worst sort of people often

de cunctis fortunae muneribus dignius existimari potest, quae ad improbissimum quemque uberiora perveniunt. De quibus illud etiam considerandum puto, quod nemo dubitat esse fortem, cui fortitudinem inesse conspexerit, et cuicumque velocitas adest manifestum est esse velocem. Sic musica quidem musicos, medicina medicos, rhetorice rhetores facit. Agit enim cuiusque rei natura quod proprium est nec contrariarum rerum miscetur effectibus et ultro quae sunt aversa depellit.

"Atqui nec opes inexpletam restinguere avaritiam queunt nec potestas sui compotem fecerit quem vitiosae libidines insolubilibus adstrictum retinent catenis, et collata improbis dignitas non modo non efficit dignos, sed prodit potius et ostentat indignos. Cur ita provenit? Gaudetis enim res sese aliter habentes falsis compellare nominibus quae facile ipsarum rerum redarguuntur effectu; itaque nec illae divitiae nec illa potentia nec haec dignitas iure appellari potest. Postremo idem de tota concludere fortuna licet in qua nihil expetendum, nihil nativae bonitatis inesse manifestum est, quae nec se bonis semper adiungit et bonos quibus fuerit adiuncta non efficit."

do hold political office, it's clear that there is no natural good in these offices because they allow themselves to be joined to evil men. Indeed we can see the same thing even more clearly in all the gifts of Fortune that pour down on the most wicked people. Consider also that no one doubts a man is strong if they see strength within him, just as whoever has swiftness is clearly swift. Likewise music makes someone musical, medicine makes someone medical, and oratory makes an orator. The nature of each skill causes what is appropriate to it and does not allow itself to be mixed with opposite causes but instead drives these opposites away.

"Wealth cannot quench insatiable greed nor can power give anyone self-control if he is bound by the unbreakable chains of evil desires. High office does not make unrighteous people honorable but instead demonstrates clearly how dishonorable they are. You mortals enjoy giving false names to things that are opposites when they are clearly contradicted by the effects of the things themselves. Thus your riches cannot rightly be called riches, nor your power be called power, nor your honor called honor. The same holds true regarding Fortune as a whole, for there is nothing in her worth seeking, nothing innately good. Fortune does not always join herself to good people nor does she make good those to whom she is joined."

Tum ego: "Scis," inquam, "ipsa minimum nobis ambitionem mortalium rerum fuisse dominatam. Sed materiam gerendis rebus optavimus quo ne virtus tacita consenesceret."

Et illa: "Atqui hoc unum est quod praestantes quidem natura mentes sed nondum ad extremam manum virtutum perfectione perductas allicere possit, gloriae scilicet cupido et optimorum in rem publicam fama meritorum; quae quam sit exilis et totius vacua ponderis, sic considera.

"Omnem terrae ambitum, sicuti astrologicis demonstrationibus accepisti, ad caeli spatium puncti constat obtinere rationem, id est ut, si ad caelestis globi magnitudinem conferatur, nihil spatii prorsus habere iudicetur. Huius igitur tam exiguae in mundo regionis quarta fere portio est, sicut Ptolomaeo probante didicisti, quae nobis cognitis animantibus incolatur. Huic quartae, si quantum maria paludesque premunt quantumque siti vasta regio distenditur cogitatione subtraxeris, vix angustissima inhabitandi hominibus area relinquetur. In hoc igitur minimo puncti quodam puncto circumsaepti atque conclusi de pervulganda fama, de proferendo nomine cogitatis? Aut quid habeat amplum magnificumque gloria tam angustis exiguisque limitibus artata?

Ambition

Then I replied: "You know that ambition for worldly things scarcely had any power over *me*. I sought the opportunity to engage in politics only to keep my virtue from fading away unpraised."

Then she sighed: "This is the one thing that has the power to seduce minds, which, though excellent by nature, have not yet been given the finishing touches in the perfection of virtues—I mean the desire for glory and reputation that comes from serving the state well. But consider just how empty and insubstantial such fame really is.

"As you know from the evidence of astronomers, the whole circumference of the earth is a mere point in comparison to the vastness of the heavens.[26] That is, if the earth were compared to the magnitude of the celestial sphere, it would be judged as taking up no space at all. And this tiny dot in a vast universe has only about a quarter of its surface inhabited by living creatures known to us, as Ptolemy argues.[27] From this inhabitable zone, subtract the amount covered by seas and swamps, as well as the vast regions of arid deserts, and scarcely will even the smallest area remain in which humans might dwell. So all of you who are hemmed into this tiny point on a point, as it were, why do you worry about trying to spread your fame about and make your name

"Adde quod hoc ipsum brevis habitaculi saeptum plures incolunt nationes lingua, moribus, totius vitae ratione distantes, ad quas tum difficultate itinerum tum loquendi diversitate tum commercii insolentia non modo fama hominum singulorum sed ne urbium quidem pervenire queat.

"Aetate denique Marci Tullii, sicut ipse quodam loco significat, nondum Caucasum montem Romanae rei publicae fama transcenderat, et erat tunc adulta Parthis etiam ceterisque id locorum gentibus formidolosa. Videsne igitur quam sit angusta, quam compressa gloria quam dilatare ac propagare laboratis? An ubi Romani nominis transire fama nequit, Romani hominis gloria progredietur? Quid quod diversarum gentium mores inter se atque instituta discordant, ut quod apud alios laude apud alios supplicio dignum iudicetur. Quod fit ut si quem famae praedicatio delectat, huic in plurimos populos nomen proferre nullo modo conducat. Erit igitur pervagata inter suos gloria quisque contentus et intra unius gentis terminos praeclara illa famae immortalitas coartabitur.

renowned? What kind of abundant and magnificent glory could you have confined as you are into such a narrow and limited area?

"Remember too that a great many nations inhabit this very small enclosure,[28] differing from each other in language, customs, and their entire way of life. Because of difficulties traveling great distances, the diversity of languages, and infrequent commerce between different nations, the fame not only of a single person but even of entire cities cannot reach them.[29]

"Finally, in the time of Marcus Tullius Cicero, as he himself writes somewhere or other, the fame of the Roman Republic had not yet spread beyond the Caucasus, even though it was in its prime and feared by the Parthians and surrounding nations.[30] So do you see, Boethius, how narrow, how confined the glory is that you all work so hard to increase and spread? Will the fame of a single Roman reach lands where the name and reputation of Rome itself is not known? And what of the fact that the customs and institutions of different peoples are at odds with one another, so that what some consider worthy of praise others deem fit for punishment? This is why even if someone delights in being praised, it doesn't at all profit him to have his name known among many people. Therefore each man should be content with glory only among his own people

"Sed quam multos clarissimos suis temporibus viros scriptorum inops delevit oblivio! Quamquam quid ipsa scripta proficiant, quae cum suis auctoribus premit longior atque obscura vetustas? Vos vero inmortalitatem vobis propagare videmini, cum futuri famam temporis cogitatis. Quod si aeternitatis infinita spatia pertractes, quid habes quod de nominis tui diuturnitate laeteris? Unius etenim mora momenti, si decem milibus conferatur annis, quoniam utrumque spatium definitum est, minimam, licet, habet tamen aliquam portionem. At hic ipse numerus annorum eiusque quamlibet multiplex ad interminabilem diuturnitatem ne comparari quidem potest. Etenim finitis ad se invicem fuerit quaedam, infiniti vero atque finiti nulla umquam poterit esse collatio. Ita fit ut quamlibet prolixi temporis fama, si cum inexhausta aeternitate cogitetur, non parva sed plane nulla esse videatur.

"Vos autem nisi ad populares auras inanesque rumores recte facere nescitis et relicta conscientiae virtutisque praestantia de alienis praemia sermunculis postulatis. Accipe in huiusmodi arrogantiae levitate quam festive aliquis inluserit.

and have his supposedly distinguished and immortal fame confined within the boundaries of his land.

"How many men, so famous in their own time, have been forgotten because of a scarcity of historians to write about them? And what good would such histories do in any case since the passing ages have wiped them away along with their writers? Yet you all seem to believe you're creating your own immortality whenever you ponder your reputations for the future. But if you were to truly consider the infinite span of eternity, what reason would you have to delight in making your name known any longer? It's true that the length of a single moment, if it's compared to ten thousand years, takes up some fragment of that time, however minuscule, since both are finite. But even ten thousand years or any multiple of it cannot be compared to a length of time that has no end. For while there can be some relationship of duration of time for finite terms, you cannot compare the finite to the infinite. And so fame, no matter how long it lasts, seems not just small but nonexistent when compared to inexhaustible eternity.

"But you humans, you don't know how to act rightly except when you're chasing after fleeting popularity and empty fame. You have abandoned the excellence of your own conscience and virtue to seek your reward from the common gossip of

"Nam cum quidam adortus esset hominem contumeliis, qui non ad verae virtutis usum sed ad superbam gloriam falsum sibi philosophi nomen induerat, adiecissetque iam se sciturum, an ille philosophus esset, si quidem illatas iniurias leniter patienterque tolerasset, ille patientiam paulisper adsumpsit acceptaque contumelia velut insultans: 'Iam tandem,' inquit, 'intellegis me esse philosophum?' Tum ille nimium mordaciter: 'Intellexeram,' inquit, 'si tacuisses.'

"Quid autem est quod ad praecipuos viros, de his enim sermo est, qui virtute gloriam petunt, quid, inquam, est quod ad hos de fama post resolutum morte suprema corpus attineat? Nam si, quod nostrae rationes credi vetant, toti moriuntur homines, nulla est omnino gloria, cum is cuius ea esse dicitur non exstet omnino. Sin vero bene sibi mens conscia terreno carcere resoluta caelum libera petit, nonne omne terrenum negotium spernat quae se caelo fruens terrenis gaudet exemptam?

others. Listen now to the story of how someone cleverly mocked the shallowness of this sort of arrogance:

"Once there was a certain person who harshly criticized another because that man had clothed himself in the name of a philosopher, not because he was seeking true virtue but because of his vanity and false pride. The one criticizing added that he would now know whether the man was a true philosopher if he bore the insults that had just been hurled at him with mildness and patience. The false philosopher reluctantly accepted the insults for a little while, then said, 'Now do you think I'm a philosopher?' The other man replied with biting sarcasm, 'I would have, if only you had kept quiet.'

"What is it that the most excellent of people—for this is the type we're speaking of, those who seek glory in virtue—what, I say, do they get from fame after the body is destroyed by death in the end? For if—though reason forbids us to believe this—human beings utterly perish, then their glory also vanishes completely since the person to whom it was said to belong no longer exists in any way. But if the mind survives conscious of its own excellence when it is freed from its earthly prison, then wouldn't it leave behind all earthly matters and happily fly to the heavens free from the things of this world?

"Sed ne me inexorabile contra fortunam gerere bellum putes, est aliquando cum de hominibus illa, fallax illa nihil, bene mereatur, tum scilicet cum se aperit, cum frontem detegit moresque profitetur.

"Nondum forte quid loquar intellegis. Mirum est quod dicere gestio, eoque sententiam verbis explicare vix queo. Etenim plus hominibus reor adversam quam prosperam prodesse fortunam. Illa enim semper specie felicitatis cum videtur blanda, mentitur; haec semper vera est, cum se instabilem mutatione demonstrat. Illa fallit, haec instruit, illa mendacium specie bonorum mentes fruentium ligat, haec cognitione fragilis felicitatis absolvit. Itaque illam videas ventosam, fluentem suique semper ignaram, hanc sobriam succinctamque et ipsius adversitatis exercitatione prudentem. Postremo felix a vero bono devios blanditiis trahit, adversa plerumque ad vera bona reduces unco retrahit.

"An hoc inter minima aestimandum putas quod amicorum tibi fidelium mentes haec aspera, haec horribilis fortuna detexit, haec tibi certos sodalium

The Uses of Fortune

"But so you don't think I'm waging a relentless war against Fortune, there is in fact a time when she's not deceitful at all but deserves respect from people. I mean when she reveals herself, takes off her mask, and shows her true ways.

"But perhaps you don't yet understand what I'm saying. The idea I'm trying to explain is a kind of paradox, so I'm hardly able to put my thought into words. Fortune, I think, is more useful for people when she is bad than when she is good. When she seems good, Fortune wears a smiling face and lies. Bad Fortune on the other hand is always honest since she shows her instability by changing. Good Fortune deceives, but bad Fortune instructs. With her false treasures, good Fortune enslaves the minds of those enjoying them, while bad Fortune frees those minds through recognition of how fragile their happiness is. You see good Fortune as inconstant, changing, always ignorant of herself, but bad Fortune is sober, prepared, and made wise by the experience of adversity. Happy Fortune lures people off the path of true good with her kisses, but adverse Fortune drags them back with her hook.

"Or perhaps you think it should be counted as a small thing that misfortune has revealed to you the hearts of friends still faithful to you? Bad Fortune

vultus ambiguosque secrevit, discedens suos abstulit, tuos reliquit? Quanti hoc integer, ut videbaris tibi fortunatus, emisses! Nunc et amissas opes querere; quod pretiosissimum divitiarum genus est amicos invenisti."

has shown to you the faces of friends loyal to you as well as those false friends who followed her when she turned away. When you were still intact[31] and, as it seemed to you, a fortunate man, how much would you have paid for this knowledge? Go on now, complain about your lost riches if you want, but you have discovered your true friends—the greatest kind of treasure."

INCIPIT LIBER III

Iam cantum illa finiverat, cum me audiendi avidum stupentemque arrectis adhuc auribus carminis mulcedo defixerat.

Itaque paulo post: "O," inquam, "summum lassorum solamen animorum quam tu me vel sententiarum pondere vel canendi etiam iucunditate refovisti! Adeo ut iam me post haec inparem fortunae ictibus esse non arbitrer. Itaque remedia quae paulo acriora esse dicebas, non modo non perhorresco, sed audiendi avidus vehementer efflagito."

Tum illa: "Sensi," inquit, "cum verba nostra tacitus attentusque rapiebas, eumque tuae mentis habitum vel exspectavi vel, quod est verius, ipsa perfeci. Talia sunt quippe quae restant, ut degustata quidem mordeant, interius autem recepta dulcescant. Sed quod tu te audiendi cupidum dicis, quanto ardore flagrares, si quonam te ducere aggrediamur agnosceres!"

BOOK 3
True Happiness

She finished singing, but the sweetness of her song still held me enchanted with my ears eager to hear more.

After a little while I spoke: "You are truly the greatest consolation for weary spirits. You have brought warmth back to my heart by the power of your arguments and even more by the delights of your singing. Even now I feel I am a match for the blows of Fortune that may yet come. And so those remedies you mentioned a little while ago saying they were more bitter, not only am I no longer terrified of them, but indeed I long to hear them."

Then she replied: "I thought so. While you were silent and attentive, grabbing hold of my every word, I was waiting for this change of heart—or to be more precise, this change I have brought about. This is in truth the nature of the remedies that remain: They are bitter when you swallow them but grow sweet once deep inside. But you say you're eager to hear more? Well, with what a fever of

"Quonam?" inquam.

"Ad veram," inquit, "felicitatem, quam tuus quoque somniat animus, sed occupato ad imagines visu ipsam illam non potest intueri."

Tum ego: "Fac obsecro et quae illa vera sit, sine cunctatione demonstra."

"Faciam," inquit illa, "tui causa libenter. Sed quae tibi [causa][3] notior est, eam prius designare verbis atque informare conabor ut ea perspecta cum in contrariam partem flexeris oculos, verae beatitudinis speciem possis agnoscere."

Tum defixo paululum visu et velut in augustam suae mentis sedem recepta sic coepit:

"Omnis mortalium cura quam multiplicium studiorum labor exercet, diverso quidem calle procedit, sed ad unum tamen beatitudinis finem nititur pervenire. Id autem est bonum quo quis adepto nihil ulterius desiderare queat. Quod quidem est omnium summum bonorum cunctaque intra se bona

desire you would burn if you only realized where I'm going to lead you!"

"Where?" I asked.

"To true happiness,"[1] she said. "This is the happiness your soul dreams of, but since your sight has been directed so far only to mere images,[2] you haven't been able to see it."

Then I said: "Do this, I beg you, and do not delay. Show me what true happiness is."

"I'll do this for you gladly," she said, "but first I'll try to describe and sketch out in words the kind of happiness that is more familiar to you, so that after you've seen it clearly, you'll be able to turn your eyes in the opposite direction and know the appearance of true blessedness."

Five False Paths to Happiness

For a little while after this she gazed at the ground as if she had withdrawn into the solemn recesses of her own mind. Then she began to speak:

"All the concerns of mortals that drive them to labor in so many different ways along various paths come down to a single goal: true happiness. When they acquire this one good thing, there's nothing more for them to desire. It's in fact the highest of all good things and all other good things are

contininens, cui si quid aforet summum esse non posset, quoniam relinqueretur extrinsecus quod posset optari. Liquet igitur esse beatitudinem statum bonorum omnium congregatione perfectum. Hunc, uti diximus, diverso tramite mortales omnes conantur adipisci. Est enim mentibus hominum veri boni naturaliter inserta cupiditas, sed ad falsa devius error abducit.

"Quorum quidem alii summum bonum esse nihilo indigere credentes ut divitiis affluant elaborant; alii vero bonum quod sit dignissimum veneratione iudicantes adeptis honoribus reverendi civibus suis esse nituntur. Sunt qui summum bonum in summa potentia esse constituant; hi vel regnare ipsi volunt vel regnantibus adhaerere conantur. At quibus optimum quiddam claritas videtur, hi vel belli vel pacis artibus gloriosum nomen propagare festinant. Plurimi vero boni fructum gaudio laetitiaque metiuntur; hi felicissimum putant voluptate diffluere. Sunt etiam qui horum fines causasque alterutro permutent, ut qui divitias ob potentiam voluptatesque desiderant vel qui potentiam seu pecuniae causa seu proferendi nominis appetunt.

contained within it. For if anything were lacking in it, it couldn't be the highest good since there would remain something outside of it to be hoped for. It's clear therefore that true happiness is a state brought about by the coming together of all good things. Now, as I have said, every person tries to acquire happiness in different ways. The desire for this true good has been naturally planted in human minds, but deceitful error leads them astray to things that are false.

"Some people think that the highest good is to lack nothing, so they work hard to have an abundance of riches. Others think the highest good is whatever brings them the most respect, so they struggle for political honors in hope of being admired by their fellow citizens. Some think the highest good resides in power, so they desire to rule or try to attach themselves to those who rule. Some think that fame is the highest good, so they try to earn a glorious name through the arts of war or peace. But most people measure the fruit of goodness by enjoyment and delight, thinking the greatest happiness comes from abandoning themselves to physical pleasure. Of course some people switch these causes and effects around so that, for example, they seek after wealth for the sake of power or physical pleasure or they desire power so that they might acquire money or make a name for themselves.

"In his igitur ceterisque talibus humanorum actuum votorumque versatur intentio, veluti nobilitas favorque popularis quae videntur quandam claritudinem comparare, uxor ac liberi quae iucunditatis gratia petuntur; amicorum vero quod sanctissimum quidem genus est, non in fortuna sed in virtute numeratur, reliquum vero vel potentiae causa vel delectationis assumitur.

"Iam vero corporis bona promptum est ut ad superiora referantur. Robur enim magnitudoque videtur praestare valentiam, pulchritudo atque velocitas celebritatem, salubritas voluptatem; quibus omnibus solam beatitudinem desiderari liquet. Nam quod quisque prae ceteris petit, id summum esse iudicat bonum. Sed summum bonum beatitudinem esse definivimus; quare beatum esse iudicat statum quem prae ceteris quisque desiderat.

"Habes igitur ante oculos propositam fere formam felicitatis humanae—opes, honores, potentiam, gloriam, voluptates. Quae quidem sola considerans Epicurus consequenter sibi summum bonum voluptatem esse constituit, quod cetera omnia iucunditatem animo videantur afferre.

"And so it is in these and similar goals that the aim of human activities and desires is found, such as nobility or the favor of the common people, both of which seem to give a certain renown, or a wife and children sought for the sake of the joy they bring. But friendship is an exception and indeed in its purest form should be numbered not with Fortune but with Virtue, for all other things are cultivated for the sake of power or pleasure.[4]

"And of course qualities of the body can also be compared to those things mentioned above. Strength and size seem to provide a person power; beauty and speed give fame; and health yields pleasure. In all of this it's clear that the one thing everyone is looking for is true happiness, because whatever people seek above all else, that is what they judge to be the highest good. But we've already defined the highest good to be true happiness, therefore each of us believes whatever thing we most desire will lead us to this type of happiness.

"And so you now have set before your eyes, as it were, the qualities that humans think bring them happiness: wealth, honors, power, glory, and pleasure. Epicurus,[5] looking at just these qualities, determined that for him the greatest good was pleasure since all the others seem to bring pleasure to the mind.

"Sed ad hominum studia revertor, quorum animus etsi caligante memoria tamen bonum suum repetit, sed velut ebrius domum quo tramite revertatur ignorat. Num enim videntur errare hi qui nihilo indigere nituntur? Atqui non est aliud quod aeque perficere beatitudinem possit quam copiosus bonorum omnium status nec alieni egens sed sibi ipse sufficiens. Num vero labuntur hi qui quod sit optimum, id etiam reverentiae cultu dignissimum putent? Minime. Neque enim vile quiddam contemnendumque est quod adipisci omnium fere mortalium laborat intentio. An in bonis non est numeranda potentia? Quid igitur? Num imbecillum ac sine viribus aestimandum est, quod omnibus rebus constat esse praestantius? An claritudo nihili pendenda est? Sed sequestrari nequit quin omne quod excellentissimum sit id etiam videatur esse clarissimum. Nam non esse anxiam tristemque beatitudinem nec doloribus molestiisque subiectam quid attinet dicere, quando in minimis quoque rebus id appetitur quod habere fruique delectet?

"Atqui haec sunt quae adipisci homines volunt eaque de causa divitias, dignitates, regna, gloriam voluptatesque desiderant quod per haec sibi sufficientiam, reverentiam, potentiam, celebritatem, laetitiam credunt esse venturam. Bonum est igitur quod tam diversis studiis homines petunt; in quo quanta sit naturae vis facile monstratur, cum licet

"But to return to the pursuits of mortals, even if the mind is cloudy it still seeks its own good, though like a drunk man it may not be able to find the path home. But are people truly wrong if they seem to lack nothing? For surely there is nothing so likely to bring about true happiness than a condition in which we have all good things and do not need anything outside of what we possess. Are people mistaken if they think that whatever is best is also most worthy of respect? Not at all. Nor is it a worthless thing that almost all mortals are striving to achieve this goal. Or should power not be numbered among the list of good things? If we do that, don't we reckon as weak and impotent that which everyone agrees is superior to other things? Or can fame be counted as nothing? But we can't ignore that what is most excellent also indeed seems to be most famous. And shouldn't we add that true happiness is not anxious or sad, not subject to sorrows or pain? For even in small things people seek what is pleasing and enjoyable.

"These then are surely the things people want to gain—wealth, honors, power, glory, and pleasure—because they think that through these things they will acquire sufficiency, respect, power, fame, and delight. It is therefore ultimately the Good[6] that people are seeking for themselves through many different pathways. In all this we can

variae dissidentesque sententiae tamen in diligendo boni fine consentiunt.

"Vos quoque, o terrena animalia, tenui licet imagine vestrum tamen principium somniatis verumque illum beatitudinis finem licet minime perspicaci qualicumque tamen cogitatione prospicitis eoque vos et ad verum bonum naturalis ducit intentio et ab eodem multiplex error abducit.

"Considera namque an per ea quibus se homines adepturos beatitudinem putant ad destinatum finem valeant pervenire. Si enim vel pecuniae vel honores ceteraque tale quid afferunt cui nihil bonorum abesse videatur, nos quoque fateamur fieri aliquos horum adeptione felices. Quod si neque id valent efficere quod promittunt bonisque pluribus carent, nonne liquido falsa in eis beatitudinis species deprehenditur?

"Primum igitur te ipsum qui paulo ante divitiis affluebas, interrogo: inter illas abundantissimas opes numquamne animum tuum concepta ex qualibet iniuria confudit anxietas?"

easily see how great the power of nature is, for although people disagree and opinions vary so much, still they all seek the Good as their ultimate goal.

Wealth Cannot Bring True Happiness

"And you also, earthly creatures, you dream of your origins even though the image you see is like a shadow. You envision the true goal of happiness with your limited imaginations, seeing it indeed, but only faintly. And so your natural inclination points you toward the true good, yet your various errors lead you away from it.

"But consider now whether people are actually able to reach their desired goal by gaining the things they think will bring them happiness. If money or honors or such things do bring about a condition in which nothing seems to be lacking, then I would admit that some people do find happiness by securing these things. But if these things fail to give what they promise and are lacking in goods, then wouldn't we have to admit that the image of true happiness in them is false?

"And so I ask you—since until recently *you* were wealthy—in the midst of all your abundant riches, was there ever a time when your mind was troubled because you felt something was wrong?"

"Atqui," inquam, "libero me fuisse animo quin aliquid semper angerer reminisci non queo."

"Nonne quia vel aberat quod abesse non velles vel aderat quod adesse noluisses?"

"Ita est," inquam.

"Illius igitur praesentiam huius absentiam desiderabas?"

"Confiteor," inquam.

"Eget vero," inquit, "eo quod quisque desiderat?"

"Eget," inquam.

"Qui vero eget aliquo, non est usquequaque sibi ipse sufficiens?"

"Minime," inquam.

"Tu itaque hanc insufficientiam plenus," inquit, "opibus sustinebas?"

"Quidni?" inquam.

"Opes igitur nihilo indigentem sufficientemque sibi facere nequeunt et hoc erat quod promittere videbantur. Atqui hoc quoque maxime considerandum puto quod nihil habeat suapte natura pecunia ut his a quibus possidetur invitis nequeat auferri."

"Fateor," inquam.

"Quidni fateare, cum eam cotidie valentior aliquis eripiat invito? Unde enim forenses querimoniae nisi

"Truly," I said, "I can't remember a time when my mind was free from worry about something or other."

"Wasn't it because you were missing something you wanted or because you had something you didn't want?"

"Yes," I said.

"You wanted the presence of something or the absence of something else?"

"Yes, I admit that," I said.

"Now don't people desire what they don't have?" she asked.

"Yes," I said.

"And a person lacking in something isn't self-sufficient in every way?"

"No indeed," I replied.

"And did you, being full of riches, ever feel this insufficiency?" she asked.

"How could I not?" I said.

"So riches cannot make a person self-sufficient and lacking in nothing, which was what they seemed to promise. And we should also consider that there is nothing in the nature of money itself that prevents it from being taken away from those who possess it against their will."

"I'll admit that," I said.

"How could you not, since every day somebody stronger seizes it from someone against his will? For

quod vel vi vel fraude nolentibus pecuniae repetuntur ereptae?"

"Ita est," inquam.

"Egebit igitur," inquit, "extrinsecus petito praesidio quo suam pecuniam quisque tueatur?"

"Quis id," inquam, "neget?"

"Atqui non egeret eo, nisi possideret pecuniam quam posset amittere?"

"Dubitari," inquam, "nequit."

"In contrarium igitur relapsa res est; nam quae sufficientes sibi facere putabantur opes, alieno potius praesidio faciunt indigentes. Quis autem modus est quo pellatur divitiis indigentia? Num enim divites esurire nequeunt? Num sitire non possunt? Num frigus hibernum pecuniosorum membra non sentiunt? Sed adest, inquies, opulentis quo famem satient, quo sitim frigusque depellant. Sed hoc modo consolari quidem divitiis indigentia potest, auferri penitus non potest. Nam si haec hians semper atque aliquid poscens opibus expletur, maneat necesse est quae possit expleri. Taceo quod naturae minimum, quod avaritiae nihil satis est. Quare si opes nec submovere possunt indigentiam et ipsae suam faciunt, quid est quod eas sufficientiam praestare credatis?

where do legal battles originate except from people trying to get back wealth taken away from them by force or fraud?"

"That's true," I answered.

"Therefore," she said, "everyone needs some sort of outside help to protect their money?"

"Who could deny that?" I admitted.

"And yet they wouldn't need help if they didn't have money they could lose?"

"That can't be doubted," I said.

"So the situation has in fact reversed itself. The riches that were supposed to make people self-sufficient have in fact made them dependent on the protection of someone else. But in what way are riches supposed to banish need? Don't rich people still need to eat? Don't they get thirsty? Don't the limbs of the wealthy feel the cold of winter? But you might reply that at least the rich have the means to satisfy their hunger or drive away thirst or cold. But although basic needs might be satisfied by money, wealth cannot remove the need deep within. For even if this need can be satisfied in some ways by riches, it is always hungry and demanding and cannot get enough. I won't even mention that nature requires very little, but greed can never be satisfied. So if wealth can't eliminate need and in fact creates its own needs, why do you mortals think that it can offer you self-sufficiency?"

"Sed dignitates honorabilem reverendumque cui provenerint reddunt. Num vis ea est magistratibus ut utentium mentibus virtutes inserant vitia depellant? Atqui non fugare sed illustrare potius nequitiam solent; quo fit ut indignemur eas saepe nequissimis hominibus contigisse, unde Catullus licet in curuli Nonium sedentem strumam tamen appellat. Videsne quantum malis dedecus adiciant dignitates? Atqui minus eorum patebit indignitas, si nullis honoribus inclarescant.

"Tu quoque num tandem tot periculis adduci potuisti ut cum Decorato gerere magistratum putares, cum in eo mentem nequissimi scurrae delatorisque respiceres? Non enim possumus ob honores reverentia dignos iudicare quos ipsis honoribus iudicamus indignos. At si quem sapientia praeditum videres, num posses eum vel reverentia vel ea qua est praeditus sapientia non dignum putare? Minime. Inest enim dignitas propria virtuti, quam protinus in eos quibus fuerit adiuncta transfundit. Quod quia populares facere nequeunt honores, liquet eos propriam dignitatis pulchritudinem non habere.

High Offices Do Not Bring Respect

"It is said that high political offices bring honor and respect to those who attain them. But surely there isn't any power in the offices themselves that plants virtues in the minds of those serving in them or drives vices away? In fact, political offices are more likely to bring wickedness to light than expel it. This is why we so often become indignant when these positions fall to the worst men, as when Catullus calls Nonius a wart[7] even though he sat in the magistrate's chair. So do you see what shame high offices bring to evil men? Their wickedness would be much less evident if they hadn't been made famous by political recognition.

"As for you, Boethius, would any number of threats have compelled you to serve alongside Decoratus when you saw he was a thoroughly wicked buffoon as well as an informer?[8] We can't very well believe that someone is worthy of respect because of their political service if we judge them unworthy of holding office in the first place. But if you saw someone endowed with wisdom, surely you wouldn't think him unworthy of respect or unworthy of that wisdom he possessed, would you? Of course not. For there is a worthiness appropriate to virtue that flows into someone who possesses that virtue. But this isn't true of political offices, so it's

"In quo illud est animadvertendum magis. Nam si eo abiectior est quo magis a pluribus quisque contemnitur, cum reverendos facere nequeat quos pluribus ostentat, despectiores potius improbos dignitas facit. Verum non impune; reddunt namque improbi parem dignitatibus vicem quas sua contagione commaculant.

"Atque ut agnoscas veram illam reverentiam per has umbratiles dignitates non posse contingere, si qua multiplici consulatu functus in barbaras nationes forte devenerit, venerandumne barbaris honor faciet? Atqui si hoc naturale munus dignitatibus foret, ab officio suo quoquo gentium nullo modo cessarent, sicut ignis ubique terrarum numquam tamen calere desistit, sed quoniam id eis non propria vis sed hominum fallax adnectit opinio, vanescunt ilico, cum ad eos venerint qui dignitates eas esse non aestimant.

"Sed hoc apud exteras nationes. Inter eos vero apud quos ortae sunt, num perpetuo perdurant? Atqui praetura magna olim potestas nunc inane nomen et senatorii census gravis sarcina; si quis

clear that they don't have the beauty that belongs to worthiness.

"In this matter there is another thing we should consider. If someone becomes more despicable when they are despised by more people, then wicked men can't become more respected when seen by more people—just the opposite. Political service in fact makes them more reviled. Neither do the offices themselves escape degrading since wicked men return an equal favor to them by contaminating them with their own disease.

"And just so you can know that true respect cannot come from shadowy[9] high offices, consider if you would a man who has served as a Roman consul many times traveling by chance to a foreign land. Would his high office make him respected by these foreigners? If high offices had by their very nature this gift to bestow, they would have this power among all nations, just as fire doesn't cease to be hot anywhere in the world. But since this power does not belong to high offices but is granted by the false opinion of men, offices become meaningless once someone travels among a people who don't count them as anything at all.

"I speak about foreign nations, but doesn't the same hold true among the people who granted the offices since nothing lasts forever? Once a praetor held great power, but now it is just an empty title

populi quondam curasset annonam, magnus habebatur, nunc ea praefectura quid abiectius? Ut enim paulo ante diximus, quod nihil habet proprii decoris, opinione utentium nunc splendorem accipit nunc amittit.

"Si igitur reverendos facere nequeunt dignitates, si ultro improborum contagione sordescunt, si mutatione temporum splendere desinunt, si gentium aestimatione vilescunt, quid est quod in se expetendae pulchritudinis habeant, nedum aliis praestent?

"An vero regna regumque familiaritas efficere potentem valet? Quidni, quando eorum felicitas perpetuo perdurat? Atqui plena est exemplorum vetustas, plena etiam praesens aetas, qui reges felicitatem calamitate mutaverint. O praeclara potentia quae ne ad conservationem quidem sui satis efficax invenitur!

"Quod si haec regnorum potestas beatitudinis auctor est, nonne si qua parte defuerit, felicitatem

and a heavy burden for a senator.[10] Once when a man was in charge of the public grain supply he was thought of as great, but now is there anything lower than this office?[11] For as I said a little while ago, a thing that has no inherent beauty waxes and wanes in splendor according to the opinion people hold of the one using it.

"And so, if high offices are not able to make anyone respected, if they are defiled by the wicked people who hold them, if they cease to be splendid because of the passage of time, and if they are worthless in the estimation of foreign nations, what attractiveness do they possess within themselves that you should seek, to say nothing of what they offer others?

True Power Does Not Belong to Kings

"But can kingdoms or friendship with kings give someone power?[12] Why not, since they surely give happiness that lasts forever? But indeed history is full of examples—as is the present age—of kings who exchanged their happiness for misery. Such a marvelous power, not even strong enough to preserve itself!

"Now if power over kingdoms is a source of true happiness, wouldn't it be the case that, if that

minuat, miseriam inportet? Sed quamvis late humana tendantur imperia, plures necesse est gentes relinqui quibus regum quisque non imperet. Qua vero parte beatos faciens desinit potestas, hac inpotentia subintrat quae miseros facit; hoc igitur modo maiorem regibus inesse necesse est miseriae portionem. Expertus sortis suae periculorum tyrannus regni metus pendentis supra verticem gladii terrore simulavit.

"Quae est igitur haec potestas quae sollicitudinum morsus expellere, quae formidinum aculeos vitare nequit? Atqui vellent ipsi vixisse securi, sed nequeunt; dehinc de potestate gloriantur. An tu potentem censes quem videas velle quod non possit efficere? Potentem censes qui satellite latus ambit, qui quos terret ipse plus metuit, qui ut potens esse videatur, in servientium manu situm est?

"Nam quid ego de regum familiaribus disseram, cum regna ipsa tantae inbecillitatis plena demonstrem? Quos quidem regia potestas saepe incolumis saepe autem lapsa prosternit. Nero Senecam familiarem praeceptoremque suum ad eligendae mortis coegit arbitrium. Papinianum diu inter aulicos

power were limited in some way, it would diminish happiness and bring about misery? So consider that however far human kingdoms might spread, there still must remain many people ruled over by no king at all. Now wherever the power that makes kings happy reaches its limit, there a lack of power creeps in and makes them miserable. And so in this way kings necessarily have within them a greater portion of unhappiness. Once there was a tyrant who knew well the dangers of this situation and so illustrated the fear kings face by hanging a sword over someone's head.[13]

"What good is this power then that isn't able to drive away a king's anxieties or banish the sting of fear? Surely kings would like to live without such cares, but they can't. And yet they boast that they are powerful! Boethius, do you think a man is powerful if he wants to do something he can't? Do you find powerful a man who walks around with a bodyguard at his side, who is more afraid than those he terrifies, who tries to look mighty by putting his safety into the hands of his servants?

"And what then should I say about the friends of kings when I've shown that kingship itself is full of weakness? Royal power, whether still intact or when it collapses, has often brought down such people. Nero forced his own friend and teacher Seneca to choose in what manner he would die.

potentem militum gladiis Antoninus obiecit. Atqui uterque potentiae suae renuntiare voluerunt, quorum Seneca opes etiam suas tradere Neroni seque in otium conferre conatus est; sed dum ruituros moles ipsa trahit, neuter quod voluit effecit.

"Quae est igitur ista potentia quam pertimescunt habentes, quam ne cum habere velis tutus sis et cum deponere cupias vitare non possis? An praesidio sunt amici quos non virtus sed fortuna conciliat? Sed quem felicitas amicum fecit, infortunium faciet inimicum. Quae vero pestis efficacior ad nocendum quam familiaris inimicus?

"Gloria vero quam fallax saepe, quam turpis est! Unde non iniuria tragicus exclamat:

> Ὦ δόξα δόξα μυρίοισι δὴ βροτῶν
> οὐδὲν γεγῶσι βίοτον ὤγκωσας μέγαν.

Plures enim magnum saepe nomen falsis vulgi opinionibus abstulerunt; quo quid turpius excogitari

Caracalla threw Papinianus, long a powerful figure at the imperial court, to the swords of his soldiers.[14] And yet both these men had wanted to leave their power behind. Seneca had even tried to give his wealth to Nero and retire to a quiet life. But they were quickly dragged down by their own weight and neither got what he wanted.

"So I ask again—what good is this power since those having it are terrified of it? When you have it you're not safe and when you want to abandon it you can't. Will friends stand by you if they were joined to you by good fortune and not virtue? Whoever success has made your friend, misfortune will make your enemy. Truly what plague is able to hurt someone more than a friend who has become a foe?

Fame and Noble Birth Mean Nothing

"How deceitful then is fame, how shameful! And so not unjustly the tragic poet exclaims:[15]

> *O Fame, Fame, for so many thousands of mortals,*
> *worthless people, you have heaped up a great living.*

For many people have often won a great name through the false opinions of the mob—and what could be thought more shameful than that? Those

potest? Nam qui falso praedicantur, suis ipsi necesse est laudibus erubescant.

"Quae si etiam meritis conquisita sit, quid tamen sapientis adiecerit conscientiae qui bonum suum non populari rumore, sed conscientiae veritate metitur? Quod si hoc ipsum propagasse nomen pulchrum videtur, consequens est ut foedum non extendisse iudicetur. Sed cum, uti paulo ante disserui, plures gentes esse necesse sit ad quas unius fama hominis nequeat pervenire, fit ut quem tu aestimas esse gloriosum, proxima parte terrarum videatur inglorius. Inter haec vero popularem gratiam ne commemoratione quidem dignam puto, quae nec iudicio provenit nec umquam firma perdurat.

"Iam vero quam sit inane quam futtile nobilitatis nomen, quis non videat? Quae si ad claritudinem refertur, aliena est. Videtur namque esse nobilitas quaedam de meritis veniens laus parentum. Quod si claritudinem praedicatio facit, illi sint clari necesse est qui praedicantur. Quare splendidum te, si tuam non habes, aliena claritudo non efficit. Quod si quid est in nobilitate bonum, id esse arbitror solum, ut inposita nobilibus necessitudo videatur ne a maiorum virtute degeneret.

who are praised unjustly should themselves blush in disgrace at such praise.

"And even if the praise is deserved, what can that add to the self-knowledge of a wise man who measures his own worth not by popular gossip but by the truth of his conscience? But if it seems good to have one's name spread abroad, then wouldn't it be true that to not have it widely known is shameful? But as I mentioned just a little while ago, since there are many people that the fame of a single person will never reach, then it seems the one you believe to be famous has no glory at all in nearby lands. This is why I think fame isn't really worth mentioning, for it doesn't arise from sound judgment and it never lasts.

"Now who cannot see how worthless a noble family name is?[16] If it arises from fame, that fame belongs to someone else, for it seems that nobility is a kind of praise inherited from the merits of your ancestors. If being talked about creates fame, then it has to be the ones actually talked about who own this fame. So you see, if you don't have your own fame, you can't very well get it from someone else. But if there is in fact anything good in a noble family name, I think it's this: It creates an obligation to those of noble birth not to fall short of the virtue of their ancestors.

"Quid autem de corporis voluptatibus loquar quarum appetentia quidem plena est anxietatis, satietas vero poenitentiae? Quantos illae morbos, quam intolerabiles dolores quasi quendam fructum nequitiae fruentium solent referre corporibus! Quarum motus quid habeat iucunditatis, ignoro. Tristes vero esse voluptatum exitus, quisquis reminisci libidinum suarum volet, intelleget. Quae si beatos explicare possunt, nihil causae est quin pecudes quoque beatae esse dicantur quarum omnis ad explendam corporalem lacunam festinat intentio.

"Honestissima quidem coniugis foret liberorumque iucunditas, sed nimis e natura dictum est nescio quem filios invenisse tortores; quorum quam sit mordax quaecumque condicio, neque alias expertum te neque nunc anxium necesse est admonere. In quo Euripidis mei sententiam probo, qui carentem liberis infortunio dixit esse felicem.

Pleasure Does Not Bring Happiness

"And what should I say then about the pleasures of the body, since the craving for them produces so much anxiety and the satisfaction of them only regret? What dreadful diseases, what unbearable sorrows they bring to the bodies of those enjoying them—a kind of fruit of their wickedness. I don't understand what joy comes from stirring up these feelings. Whoever cares to remember their own uncontrolled desires will recall the sad end they bring. If bodily pleasures bring about true happiness, then we should call animals happy too since their whole lives are dedicated to fulfilling the needs of their bodies.

"The pleasure of having a wife and children may be a very good thing, but there's also a saying true to nature that someone invented children to be tormentors. But it's hardly necessary to remind you, Boethius, how the condition of one's children, whatever it might be, gnaws at a parent, as you experienced in your past and even now. In this I must agree with my Euripides, who says whoever lacks children is happy in his misfortune.[17]

"Nihil igitur dubium est quin hae ad beatitudinem viae devia quaedam sint nec perducere quemquam eo valeant ad quod se perducturas esse promittunt. Quantis vero implicitae malis sint, brevissime monstrabo.

"Quid enim? Pecuniamne congregare conaberis? Sed eripies habenti. Dignitatibus fulgere velis? Danti supplicabis et qui praeire ceteros honore cupis, poscendi humilitate vilesces. Potentiamne desideras? Subiectorum insidiis obnoxius periculis subiacebis. Gloriam petas? Sed per aspera quaeque distractus securus esse desistis. Voluptariam vitam degas? Sed quis non spernat atque abiciat vilissimae fragilissimaeque rei corporis servum?

"Iam vero qui bona prae se corporis ferunt, quam exigua, quam fragili possessione nituntur! Num enim elephantos mole, tauros robore superare poteritis, num tigres velocitate praeibitis? Respicite caeli spatium firmitudinem celeritatem et aliquando

None of These Things Are a Path to True Happiness

"And so there's no doubt that these paths[18] to true happiness are detours of one sort or another and are unable to lead people where they promise. I will briefly show you the kind of troubles with which they are intertwined.

"Which would you prefer? Would you like to pile up a huge fortune? But you'll have to take it from someone who has it. Do you want to shine brightly in high political offices? You'll have to bend your knee before the one granting them, so that you who desire to surpass others in honor will bring shame to yourself by begging for it. Do you want to be a king? You'll lie exposed to the plots of your subjects and submit yourself to terrible risks. Do you long for fame? You'll be dragged through every sort of difficulty and never be safe. What about a life devoted to physical pleasure? But then who wouldn't despise and reject you as a slave to the most vile and fragile of things, the human body?

"As for those who make a display of their bodies, what a puny, what a fragile thing they rely on. Surely you humans cannot surpass an elephant in size nor a bull in strength nor a tiger in speed. Look up at the vastness of the heavens, the mightiness

desinite vilia mirari. Quod quidem caelum non his potius est quam sua qua regitur ratione mirandum.

"Formae vero nitor ut rapidus est, ut velox et vernalium florum mutabilitate fugacior! Quod si, ut Aristoteles ait, Lynceis oculis homines uterentur, ut eorum visus obstantia penetraret, nonne introspectis visceribus illud Alcibiadis superficie pulcherrimum corpus turpissimum videretur? Igitur te pulchrum videri non tua natura sed oculorum spectantium reddit infirmitas. Sed aestimate quam vultis nimio corporis bona, dum sciatis hoc quodcumque miramini triduanae febris igniculo posse dissolvi!

"Ex quibus omnibus illud redigere in summam licet, quod haec quae nec praestare quae pollicentur bona possunt nec omnium bonorum congregatione perfecta sunt, ea nec ad beatitudinem quasi quidem calles ferunt nec beatos ipsa perficiunt.

of the firmament, the speed of the stars, and stop admiring worthless things. Though indeed it isn't even the heavens you should admire, but the one who rules them.

"The beauty of the body slips away so fast, so quickly it passes, more fleeting than ever-changing flowers of spring. As Aristotle says, if people had the eyes of Lynceus so that their vision could penetrate any barriers, wouldn't even the beauty of Alcibiades, the most handsome of men on the surface, look ugly after they've seen the guts beneath his skin?[19] So it isn't your own nature that makes your body seem beautiful, but the limited vision of those around you. Go ahead, mortals, prize as you will your wonderful bodies, but do remember this thing you so admire can be burned away by a three-day fever.

"So in considering all these things we've discussed, let me sum it up for you: These things cannot provide the goods they promise nor can they become perfect by bringing together all good things. They can't lead you to true happiness at the end of their various roads nor can they themselves make people truly happy.

"Hactenus mendacis formam felicitatis ostendisse suffecerit, quam si perspicaciter intueris, ordo est deinceps quae sit vera monstrare."

"Atqui video," inquam, "nec opibus sufficientiam nec regnis potentiam nec reverentiam dignitatibus nec celebritatem gloria nec laetitiam voluptatibus posse contingere."

"An etiam causas, cur id ita sit, deprehendisti?"

"Tenui quidem veluti rimula mihi videor intueri, sed ex te apertius cognoscere malim."

"Atqui promptissima ratio est. Quod enim simplex est indivisumque natura, id error humanus separat et a vero atque perfecto ad falsum imperfectumque traducit. An tu arbitraris quod nihilo indigeat egere potentia?"

"Minime," inquam.

"Recte tu quidem. Nam si quid est quod in ulla re inbecillioris valentiae sit, in hac praesidio necesse est egeat alieno."

"Ita est," inquam.

"Igitur sufficientiae potentiaeque una est eademque natura."

"Sic videtur."

True Happiness at Last

"So far it's been enough to show you a picture of false happiness. If you can see this clearly, it's now time to show you what true happiness is."[20]

"I do see," I said, "that sufficiency cannot come from wealth nor power from ruling nor respect from political office nor glory from fame nor joy from pleasing the body."

"But have you discovered the reasons why this is true?"

"I think so, but only as if I were peeking through a small crack in a wall. I'd like to learn them from you more clearly."

"The explanation is very close at hand. What is simple and indivisible in its own nature, human error divides into pieces and transforms from the true and perfect to the false and imperfect. Now do you think that something in need of nothing is lacking in power?"

"Not at all," I said.

"Right you are. For if something is lacking in power in any way, it must need the help of something else beyond it."

"That's true," I said.

"So the nature of sufficiency and of power are one and the same."

"It seems so."

"Quod vero huiusmodi sit, spernendumne esse censes an contra rerum omnium veneratione dignissimum?"

"At hoc," inquam, "ne dubitari quidem potest."

"Addamus igitur sufficientiae potentiaeque reverentiam, ut haec tria unum esse iudicemus."

"Addamus, si quidem vera volumus confiteri."

"Quid vero," inquit, "obscurumne hoc atque ignobile censes esse an omni celebritate clarissimum? Considera vero, ne quod nihilo indigere, quod potentissimum, quod honore dignissimum esse concessum est, egere claritudine quam sibi praestare non possit atque ob id aliqua ex parte videatur abiectius."

"Non possum," inquam, "quin hoc uti est ita etiam celeberrimum esse confitear."

"Consequens igitur est ut claritudinem superioribus tribus nihil differre fateamur."

"Consequitur," inquam.

"Quod igitur nullius egeat alieni, quod suis cuncta viribus possit, quod sit clarum atque reverendum, nonne hoc etiam constat esse laetissimum?"

"Sed unde huic," inquam, "tali maeror ullus obrepat ne cogitare quidem possum; quare plenum

"Then whatever has this sort of nature, should it be despised or, to the contrary, is it worthy of respect above all other things?"

"The latter," I said. "There is no doubt."

"So let us add respect to sufficiency and power, so that we may then judge these three things to be in fact one."

"Let's do add it, if we want to admit the truth."

"Well then," she said, "do you think what we've just described is obscure and undistinguished or is it famous and renowned? Consider carefully: Would something that we have judged as lacking in nothing, having immense power, and being worthy of respect need fame it can't provide for itself and therefore be disreputable in some way?"

"That wouldn't be possible," I said. "This thing we're talking about, being what it is, must be unsurpassed in fame."

"Then we must admit that fame differs in no way from the three previous things."

"That's true," I said.

"And whatever needs nothing outside of itself, can do all things by its own strength, and is both famous and respected, wouldn't it also be supremely joyous?"

"Indeed," I said, "I can't imagine from where any kind of sorrow might sneak up on such a thing. So

esse laetitiae, si quidem superiora manebunt, necesse est confiteri."

"Atqui illud quoque per eadem necessarium est sufficientiae, potentiae, claritudinis, reverentiae, iucunditatis nomina quidem esse diversa, nullo modo vero discrepare substantiam."

"Necesse est," inquam.

"Hoc igitur quod est unum simplexque natura, pravitas humana dispertit et dum rei quae partibus caret partem conatur adipisci, nec portionem quae nulla est nec ipsam quam minime affectat assequitur."

"Quonam," inquam, "modo?"

"Qui divitias," inquit, "petit penuriae fuga, de potentia nihil laborat, vilis obscurusque esse mavult, multas etiam sibi naturales quoque subtrahit voluptates, ne pecuniam quam paravit amittat. Sed hoc modo ne sufficientia quidem contingit ei quem valentia deserit, quem molestia pungit, quem vilitas abicit, quem recondit obscuritas. Qui vero solum posse desiderat, profligat opes, despicit voluptates honoremque potentia carentem gloriam quoque nihili pendit. Sed hunc quoque quam multa deficiant vides. Fit enim ut aliquando necessariis egeat, ut anxietatibus mordeatur cumque haec depellere nequeat, etiam id quod maxime petebat potens esse desistat. Similiter ratiocinari de honoribus,

I must agree that it is filled with joy, as long as the above conclusions hold."

"So it must then be necessary that sufficiency, power, fame, respect, and joy differ from each other in name but are in fact one substance."

"That's true," I said.

"This thing, therefore, that is by nature one and complete, human perversity has divided into pieces. And so when you try to gain a part of this thing that has no parts, you get neither the part—which doesn't exist—nor the whole, which is not being sought."

"How does that happen?" I asked.

"A person," she said, "who seeks wealth in a flight from poverty makes no effort to gain power. They prefer to be lowly and unknown, even robbing themselves of the natural pleasures of life, just so they don't lose the money they have acquired. But in doing so, they don't even gain the self-sufficiency they long for, since their health deserts them, trouble consumes them, squalor plagues them, and they die in obscurity. On the other hand, the ones who want only power squander wealth, avoid pleasures of the body, despise honors that come without power, and consider fame to be worthless. But you see again how many things these people lack, sometimes not even having basic necessities, and so are gnawed on

gloria, voluptatibus licet. Nam cum unumquodque horum idem quod cetera sit, quisquis horum aliquid sine ceteris petit, ne illud quidem quod desiderat apprehendit."

"Quid igitur," inquam, "si qui cuncta simul cupiat adipisci, summam quidem ille beatudinis velit?"

"Sed num in his eam reperiet, quae demonstravimus id quod pollicentur non posse conferre?"

"Minime," inquam.

"In his igitur quae singula quaedam expetendorum praestare creduntur, beatitudo nullo modo vestiganda est."

"Fateor," inquam, "et hoc nihil dici verius potest."

"Habes igitur," inquit, "et formam falsae felicitatis et causas. Deflecte nunc in adversum mentis intuitum; ibi enim veram quam promisimus statim videbis."

"Atqui haec," inquam, "vel caeco perspicua est eamque tu paulo ante monstrasti, dum falsae causas aperire conaris. Nam nisi fallor ea vera est et perfecta felicitas quae sufficientem, potentem, reverendum, celebrem laetumque perficiat. Atque ut me interius animadvertisse cognoscas, quae unum

by worry. Unable to dismiss their anxieties, they lose also that power they sought above all. You can say the same about honors, fame, and physical pleasure, for each of them is like the others. Whoever seeks one of these things without the rest misses out on even the single thing they desired most."

"So then," I said, "if someone wanted to secure them all at once, he would be seeking the whole of true happiness?"

"But he won't find it in these things, will he, since I've shown they can't deliver what they promise?"

"No, he won't," I said.

"Therefore true happiness can by no means be found in things that are believed to offer only one of the things sought?"

"I'll admit that," I said, "since nothing could be more true."

"So," she said, "you have then before you both the nature and the cause of false happiness. But now turn the gaze of your mind in the opposite direction, to the place where you will see the true happiness I promised."

"But," I said, "what this might be is obvious even to a blind man. You mentioned it just a little while ago when you were trying to reveal the causes of false happiness. For unless I'm mistaken, true and perfect happiness is that which makes a person sufficient, powerful, respected, renowned, and joyful. And just

horum, quoniam idem cuncta sunt, veraciter praestare potest hanc esse plenam beatitudinem sine ambiguitate cognosco."

"O te alumne hac opinione felicem, si quidem hoc," inquit, "adieceris."

"Quidnam?" inquam.

"Essene aliquid in his mortalibus caducisque rebus putas quod huiusmodi statum possit afferre?"

"Minime," inquam, "puto idque a te, nihil ut amplius desideretur, ostensum est."

"Haec igitur vel imagines veri boni vel inperfecta quaedam bona dare mortalibus videntur, verum autem atque perfectum bonum conferre non possunt."

"Assentior," inquam.

"Quoniam igitur agnovisti quae vera illa sit, quae autem beatitudinem mentiantur, nunc superest ut unde veram hanc petere possis agnoscas."

"Id quidem," inquam, "iam dudum vehementer exspecto."

"Sed cum, ut in Timaeo Platoni," inquit, "nostro placet, in minimis quoque rebus divinum praesidium debeat implorari, quid nunc faciendum censes, ut illius summi boni sedem reperire mereamur?"

so you'll know that I've understood this deeply in my mind, I'll say that I know without a doubt that complete happiness is that which can offer any one of these things, since they're all the same."

"O my child," she said, "how happy you would be if you would add but one thing."

"What's that?" I asked.

"Do you think there is anything in this world of mortal and transitory things that can bring about this state of true happiness?"

"Not at all," I said. "I think you've shown this well enough so that no further proofs are needed."

"So these things can only offer mortals shadows of the true good, or perhaps offer them imperfect goods, but they can't confer that true and perfect good."

"I agree," I said.

"And since you've learned what true happiness is and those things that only pretend to be, it now remains for you to learn where you can seek this true happiness."

"This is the very thing," I said, "that I've been waiting for so long."

"But since," she said, "just as my Plato says in his *Timaeus*,[21] we ought to pray for divine help even in the smallest of matters, what do you think we should do so that we might be worthy to discover the source of the highest good?"

"Invocandum," inquam, "rerum omnium patrem, quo praetermisso nullum rite fundatur exordium."

"Recte," inquit, ac simul ita modulata est.

"Quoniam igitur quae sit imperfecti, quae etiam perfecti boni forma vidisti, nunc demonstrandum reor quonam haec felicitatis perfectio constituta sit.

"In quo illud primum arbitror inquirendum, an aliquod huiusmodi bonum quale paulo ante definisti in rerum natura possit exsistere, ne nos praeter rei subiectae veritatem cassa cogitationis imago decipiat. Sed quin exsistat sitque hoc veluti quidam omnium fons bonorum negari nequit. Omne enim quod inperfectum esse dicitur, id inminutione perfecti inperfectum esse perhibetur. Quo fit, ut si in quolibet genere inperfectum quid esse videatur, in eo perfectum quoque aliquid esse necesse sit. Etenim perfectione sublata, unde illud quod inperfectum perhibetur exstiterit ne fingi quidem potest. Neque enim ab deminutis inconsummatisque natura rerum coepit exordium, sed ab integris absolutisque procedens in haec extrema atque effeta dilabitur. Quod si, uti paulo ante monstravimus, est quaedam

"We ought," I said, "to call on the father of all things, for if we omit this prayer we cannot have a proper beginning to our work."

"Indeed," she said.

True Happiness Is True Goodness

"Since you've seen the essence of both imperfect and perfect good, I think now I should show you where this perfection of happiness is found.

"Regarding this, I think we first have to ask whether it's possible for any good of the sort you defined a while ago to exist in the natural world. This is so no empty image from our thoughts deceives us and takes us away from the truth of the matter we're considering. But it must be true that such a thing exists and it can't be denied that it is, as it were, the source of good things. For everything that is said to be imperfect is considered to be so because it has a reduced perfection. So it is that if any class of things seems to be imperfect in some way, then it's necessary that there is also some perfection in it. For if you take all the perfection away from something, it's hard to imagine how something imperfect can even exist. Indeed the universe did not arise in the beginning from diminished and incomplete things but degenerated from a whole and perfect state

boni fragilis inperfecta felicitas, esse aliquam solidam perfectamque non potest dubitari."

"Firmissime," inquam, "verissimeque conclusum est."

"Quo vero," inquit, "habitet, ita considera. Deum rerum omnium principem bonum esse communis humanorum conceptio probat animorum. Nam cum nihil deo melius excogitari queat, id quo melius nihil est bonum esse quis dubitet? Ita vero bonum esse deum ratio demonstrat, ut perfectum quoque in eo bonum esse convincat. Nam ni tale sit, rerum omnium princeps esse non poterit. Erit enim eo praestantius aliquid perfectum possidens bonum, quod hoc prius atque antiquius esse videatur; omnia namque perfecta minus integris priora esse claruerunt. Quare ne in infinitum ratio prodeat, confitendum est summum deum summi perfectique boni esse plenissimum. Sed perfectum bonum veram esse beatitudinem constituimus; veram igitur beatitudinem in summo deo sitam esse necesse est."

into this exhausted and faded condition. Therefore if, as we demonstrated a little while ago, there is some imperfect happiness in a perishable good, then we can't doubt that there is also a happiness that is enduring and perfect."

"This conclusion," I said, "is very sound and absolutely true."

"But as for where this happiness exists," she said, "consider this. The common belief of human minds is that God, the author of all things, is good. For since nothing is able to be imagined that is better than God, who could doubt that something which has nothing better than it is good? Reason indeed shows that God is good in such a way that it proves perfect goodness lives within him. For if this wasn't true, he wouldn't be able to be the ruler of all things, since then there would be something possessing perfect good more excellent than God, something that would be greater and more ancient than him. For it has become clear that all things that are perfect come before those things that are less perfect. So to keep this line of reasoning from regressing infinitely, it must be admitted that God is above all and is therefore most full of the highest and most perfect good. Now we have established that the most perfect good is true happiness, therefore true happiness must dwell in this highest God."

"Accipio," inquam, "nec est quod contradici ullo modo queat."

"Sed quaeso," inquit, "te vide quam id sancte atque inviolabiliter probes quod boni summi summum deum diximus esse plenissimum."

"Quonam," inquam, "modo?"

"Ne hunc rerum omnium patrem illud summum bonum quo plenus esse perhibetur vel extrinsecus accepisse vel ita naturaliter habere praesumas, quasi habentis dei habitaeque beatitudinis diversam cogites esse substantiam. Nam si extrinsecus acceptum putes, praestantius id quod dederit ab eo quod acceperit existimare possis. Sed hunc esse rerum omnium praecellentissimum dignissime confitemur. Quod si natura quidem inest, sed est ratione diversum, cum de rerum principe loquamur deo, fingat qui potest: quis haec diversa coniunxerit? Postremo quod a qualibet re diversum est, id non est illud a quo intellegitur esse diversum. Quare quod a summo bono diversum est sui natura, id summum bonum non est—quod nefas est de eo cogitare quo nihil constat esse praestantius. Omnino enim nullius rei natura suo principio melior poterit exsistere, quare quod omnium principium sit, id etiam sui substantia summum esse bonum verissima ratione concluserim."

"I accept that," I said, "for nothing can in any way be said against it."

"But," she said, "I ask you to be solemnly and inviolably sure about what we just said, that the highest God must be most full of the highest good."

"What do you mean?" I asked.

"I mean you shouldn't think that the father of all things, who is held to be full of the highest good, received that good from outside of himself. Nor should you think that he possesses this good by nature so that the substance of God having it and the substance of the true happiness he has are separate things. For if you think he accepted this good from something outside himself, you could suppose that whatever gave it to him is more excellent than him. But we most appropriately agree that God is the most excellent of all things. But on the other hand, if true happiness is present by its own nature in God but is distinct in principle from him, then whenever we talk about God as the creator of all things, couldn't someone ask who joined these two separate things together? Finally that which is different from something else is not the same thing as that which it is understood to be different from. So that which is different in nature from the highest good is not the highest good—a wicked thing to think about God since we have agreed there is nothing more excellent than him. Since there can

"Rectissime," inquam.

"Sed summum bonum beatitudinem esse concessum est."

"Ita est," inquam.

"Igitur," inquit, "deum esse ipsam beatitudinem necesse est confiteri."

"Nec propositis," inquam, "prioribus refragari queo et illis hoc inlatum consequens esse perspicio."

"Respice," inquit, "an hinc quoque idem firmius approbetur, quod duo summa bona quae a se diversa sint esse non possunt. Etenim quae discrepant bona, non esse alterum quod sit alterum liquet; quare neutrum poterit esse perfectum, cum alterutri alterum deest. Sed quod perfectum non sit, id summum non esse manifestum est; nullo modo igitur quae summa sunt bona ea possunt esse diversa. Atqui et beatitudinem et deum summum bonum esse collegimus; quare ipsam necesse est summam esse beatitudinem quae sit summa divinitas."

"Nihil," inquam, "nec reapse verius nec ratiocinatione firmius nec deo dignius concludi potest."

exist nothing that by its own nature is superior to its source, I would conclude by this truest reasoning that which is the source of all things is by its own substance the highest good."

"Perfectly right," I said.

"But we have conceded that the highest good is happiness."

"Yes, it is," I said.

"Therefore," she said, "it must be admitted that God is happiness itself."

"I'm not able," I said, "to oppose your previous propositions, so this inference must follow from them."

"Consider also," she said, "whether we can assert the same thing more certainly from this argument as well: Two highest goods are not able to exist separately from each other. For if two goods are separate, the one is not the same as the other, thus neither is able to be perfect because one is lacking the other. But what is not perfect is clearly not the highest thing. Therefore there is no way that two highest goods are able to be different. But we have agreed that both happiness and God are a highest good, so it's necessary that the highest happiness is also the highest divinity."

"No conclusion," I said, "could indeed be made that is more true or more firmly reasoned or more worthy of God."

"Super haec," inquit, "igitur veluti geometrae solent demonstratis propositis aliquid inferre quae porismata ipsi vocant, ita ego quoque tibi veluti corollarium dabo. Nam quoniam beatitudinis adeptione fiunt homines beati, beatitudo vero est ipsa divinitas, divinitatis adeptione beatos fieri manifestum est: sed uti iustitiae adeptione iusti, sapientiae sapientes fiunt, ita divinitatem adeptos deos fieri simili ratione necesse est. Omnis igitur beatus deus, sed natura quidem unus; participatione vero nihil prohibet esse quam plurimos."

"Et pulchrum," inquam, "hoc atque pretiosum, sive porisma sive corollarium vocari mavis."

"Atqui hoc quoque pulchrius nihil est, quod his annectendum esse ratio persuadet."

"Quid?" inquam.

"Cum multa," inquit, "beatitudo continere videatur, utrumne haec omnia unum veluti corpus beatitudinis quadam partium varietate coniungant an sit eorum aliquid quod beatitudinis substantiam compleat, ad hoc vero cetera referantur?"

"In addition to these arguments," she said, "just as geometricians, after they have proven their propositions, draw from them additional conclusions they call *porismata*, I will give you a kind of corollary.[22] Since people become truly happy from the acquisition of true happiness, but true happiness is itself divinity, then it is obvious that they become truly happy by acquiring divinity. For, just as people become just by acquiring justice and wise by acquiring wisdom, it is necessary by this kind of reasoning that by acquiring divinity they become gods. Therefore every truly happy person is a god, though by nature God is one only. But nothing prevents there from being as many gods as you like by participation."[23]

"This," I said, "is a beautiful and precious idea, whether you prefer it be called a *porisma* or a corollary."

"But there is nothing more beautiful than one additional thing that must be connected to this argument."

"What?" I asked.

"Since," she said, "true happiness seems to contain many things, do all these parts join together and make, so to speak, one body of happiness or is there among them one element that makes complete the substance of true happiness and to which all the others are related?"

"Vellem," inquam, "id ipsarum rerum commemoratione patefaceres."

"Nonne," inquit, "beatitudinem bonum esse censemus?"

"Ac summum quidem," inquam.

"Addas," inquit, "hoc omnibus licet. Nam eadem sufficientia summa est, eadem summa potentia, reverentia quoque, claritas ac voluptas beatitudo esse iudicatur. Quid igitur? Haecine omnia—bonum sufficientia potentia ceteraque—veluti quaedam beatitudinis membra sunt an ad bonum veluti ad verticem cuncta referuntur?"

"Intellego," inquam, "quid investigandum proponas, sed quid constituas audire desidero."

"Cuius discretionem rei sic accipe. Si haec omnia beatitudinis membra forent, a se quoque invicem discreparent. Haec est enim partium natura ut unum corpus diversa componant. Atqui haec omnia idem esse monstrata sunt; minime igitur membra sunt. Alioquin ex uno membro beatitudo videbitur esse coniuncta—quod fieri nequit."

"Id quidem," inquam, "dubium non est, sed id quod restat exspecto."

"I would like," I said, "for you to make this question clearer by reminding me of these things themselves."

"Don't we agree," she asked, "that true happiness is good?"

"Indeed, the highest good," I said.

"You may add that," she said, "to all the other parts. For true happiness is judged to be the highest sufficiency, the highest power, the highest respect, the highest fame, and the highest pleasure. What then? Are all of these—good, sufficiency, power, and the rest—kinds of limbs of the body of true happiness, or are they all understood in relation to the good as their head, as it were?"

"I understand," I said, "what you are proposing we investigate, but I would like to hear what your conclusion is."

"So then accept the separation of the argument as follows: If all these things were limbs of true happiness, they would be distinct from one another. That is the nature of parts so that they combine diverse things to form a single body. But they have all been shown to be the same thing, so they can hardly be limbs. Otherwise true happiness will seem to be joined together from one part, which doesn't make any sense."

"Regarding that," I said, "there can be no doubt, but I'm waiting for what remains."

"Ad bonum vero cetera referri palam est. Idcirco enim sufficientia petitur quoniam bonum esse iudicatur, idcirco potentia quoniam id quoque esse creditur bonum; idem de reverentia, claritudine, iucunditate coniectare licet. Omnium igitur expetendorum summa atque causa bonum est. Quod enim neque re neque similitudine ullum in se retinet bonum, id expeti nullo modo potest. Contraque etiam quae natura bona non sunt, tamen si esse videantur, quasi vere bona sint appetuntur. Quo fit uti summa, cardo atque causa expetendorum omnium bonitas esse iure credatur. Cuius vero causa quid expetitur, id maxime videtur optari, veluti si salutis causa quispiam velit equitare, non tam equitandi motum desiderat quam salutis effectum. Cum igitur omnia boni gratia petantur, non illa potius quam bonum ipsum desideratur ab omnibus. Sed propter quod cetera optantur, beatitudinem esse concessimus; quare sic quoque sola quaeritur beatitudo. Ex quo liquido apparet ipsius boni et beatitudinis unam atque eandem esse substantiam."

"Nihil video cur dissentire quispiam possit."

"Sed deum veramque beatitudinem unum atque idem esse monstravimus."

"It is clear that all the other parts are to be understood in relation to the good. This is why sufficiency is sought, because it is good. Likewise power since it is believed to be good. The same holds true for respect, fame, and pleasure. The sum total and cause of all things sought after is the good. For that which has within itself no good either by resemblance or in reality is in no way sought after. Indeed even those things that are by nature not good but only seem to be good are sought after as if they were good. And so it is rightly believed that the sum total, the center point, and the cause of all things to be sought after is goodness. But the cause for which a thing is sought seems to be what is desired most, as when someone wishes to ride a horse for physical health, it's not the motion of the moving horse they desire but the benefit to their health. Therefore, since all things are sought for the sake of the good, it's not really those things that everyone desires but the good itself. But we have concluded that true happiness is the reason the other things are desired. In the same way true happiness is all that is sought after. From this it clearly appears that the substance of the good itself and the substance of true happiness are one and the same."

"I see no reason why anyone would disagree."

"But we have shown that God and true happiness are one and the same."

"Ita," inquam.

"Securo igitur concludere licet dei quoque in ipso bono nec usquam alio sitam esse substantiam."

"Assentior," inquam," cuncta enim firmissimis nexa rationibus constant."

Tum illa: "Quanti," inquit, "aestimabis, si bonum ipsum quid sit agnoveris?"

"Infinito," inquam, "si quidem mihi pariter deum quoque qui bonum est continget agnoscere."

"Atqui hoc verissima," inquit, "ratione patefaciam, maneant modo quae paulo ante conclusa sunt."

"Manebunt."

"Nonne," inquit, "monstravimus ea quae appetuntur pluribus idcirco vera perfectaque bona non esse quoniam a se invicem discreparent cumque alteri abesset alterum, plenum absolutumque bonum afferre non posse? Tum autem verum bonum fieri cum in unam veluti formam atque efficientiam colliguntur, ut quae sufficientia est, eadem sit potentia, reverentia, claritas atque iucunditas, nisi vero unum atque idem omnia sint, nihil habere quo inter expetenda numerentur?"

"Yes," I said.

"Therefore we may confidently conclude that the substance of God dwells in the good itself and nowhere else."

The Good and the One Are the Same

"I agree," I said. "All these points are woven together and stand by the firmest reasoning."

Then she said, "What do you think it would be worth if you can learn what the good itself is?"

"An infinite price," I said, "since at the same time I will come to know God, who is the good."

"I will make that clear too," she said, "by the truest reasoning, if indeed the conclusions we reached a little earlier still stand."

"They will stand."

"Haven't we demonstrated," she then continued, "that the things desired by most people are not true and perfect goods, since they differ from each other, and when one is absent from another they are not able to confer full and absolute good? And don't they become truly good when they are gathered together, as it were, into one form and effect, so that what sufficiency is, power is that same thing, likewise respect, fame, and joy? But unless all of these were one and the same, surely they wouldn't possess

"Demonstratum," inquam, "nec dubitari ullo modo potest."

"Quae igitur cum discrepant minime bona sunt, cum vero unum esse coeperint, bona fiunt; nonne haec ut bona sint, unitatis fieri adeptione contingit?"

"Ita," inquam, "videtur."

"Sed omne quod bonum est boni participatione bonum esse concedis an minime?"

"Ita est."

"Oportet igitur idem esse unum atque bonum simili ratione concedas; eadem namque substantia est eorum quorum naturaliter non est diversus effectus."

"Negare," inquam, "nequeo."

"Nostine igitur," inquit, "omne quod est tam diu manere atque subsistere quam diu sit unum, sed interire atque dissolvi pariter atque unum destiterit?"

"Quonam modo?"

"Ut in animalibus," inquit, "cum in unum coeunt ac permanent anima corpusque, id animal vocatur; cum vero haec unitas utriusque separatione dissolvitur, interire nec iam esse animal liquet. Ipsum quoque corpus cum in una forma membrorum coniunctione permanet, humana visitur species;

anything that would allow them to be numbered among things to be sought?"

"That," I said, "has been demonstrated and is in no way able to be doubted."

"Therefore these things that are not as completely good when they differ become so when they begin to be one. Don't these things become good by the acquisition of unity?"

"Yes," I said, "it seems so."

"But do you agree or not that everything that is good is good by participation in the good?"

"It is."

"Therefore you must also agree by similar reasoning that the one and the good are the same, for by nature they have to be the same if there is no difference in their effect."

"I am not able," I said, "to deny that."

"And as you know," she said, "everything that exists remains and has substance only as long as it is one, and that it passes away and is destroyed as soon as it ceases to be one."

"What do you mean?"

"With a living creature," she said, "when spirit and body come together and remain as one, it is called a living thing. But when this unity is dissolved by the separation of one from the other, it is clear that it perishes and is no longer a living creature. Also a body itself while its parts remain joined

at si distributae segregataeque partes corporis distraxerint unitatem, desinit esse quod fuerat. Eoque modo percurrenti cetera procul dubio patebit subsistere unumquodque, dum unum est, cum vero unum esse desinit, interire."

"Consideranti," inquam, "mihi plura minime aliud videtur."

"Estne igitur," inquit, "quod in quantum naturaliter agat relicta subsistendi appetentia venire ad interitum corruptionemque desideret?"

"Si animalia," inquam, "considerem quae habent aliquam volendi nolendique naturam, nihil invenio quod nullis extra cogentibus abiciant manendi intentionem et ad interitum sponte festinent. Omne namque animal tueri salutem laborat, mortem vero perniciemque devitat. Sed quid de herbis arboribusque, quid de inanimatis omnino consentiam rebus prorsus dubito."

"Atqui non est quod de hoc quoque possis ambigere, cum herbas atque arbores intuearis primum sibi convenientibus innasci locis, ubi quantum earum natura queat cito exarescere atque interire non possint. Nam aliae quidem campis aliae montibus oriuntur, alias ferunt paludes, aliae saxis haerent,

together as one is seen as having a human form. But if the parts of the body are divided and separated so that its unity is torn apart, then it ceases to be what it once was. In the same way, if you consider other examples, it will be clear beyond any doubt that each thing has substance as long as it is unified, but when that unity ceases it perishes."

"When I consider many other examples," I said, "it seems not in the least different."

"Is there anything then," she asked, "so far as it acts according to its own nature, that would leave behind its appetite for existence and desire for itself death and destruction?"

"If," I said, "I consider living creatures that have some natural capacity for wanting or not wanting, I can think of none that would freely cast aside their desire to remain alive and hasten their own destruction, provided there are no external forces acting on them. For every living creature strives to preserve its own well-being and avoid death and destruction. But concerning plants and trees and inanimate things, I'm not at all sure what to think."

"But there is no reason why you should be in doubt concerning them either, since first of all you can clearly see that plants and trees arise in places appropriate for them, where, in as far as their nature allows, they are not able to wither away quickly and perish. For some spring up in fields and others

aliarum fecundae sunt steriles harenae, quas si in alia quispiam loca transferre conetur, arescant. Sed dat cuique natura quod convenit et ne, dum manere possunt, intereant, elaborat.

"Quid quod omnes velut in terras ore demerso trahunt alimenta radicibus ac per medullas robur corticemque diffundunt? Quid quod mollissimum quidque, sicuti medulla est, interiore semper sede reconditur, extra vero quadam ligni firmitate, ultimus autem cortex adversum caeli intemperiem quasi mali patiens defensor opponitur? Iam vero quanta est naturae diligentia, ut cuncta semine multiplicato propagentur! Quae omnia non modo ad tempus manendi verum generatim quoque quasi in perpetuum permanendi veluti quasdam machinas esse quis nesciat?

"Ea etiam quae inanimata esse creduntur nonne quod suum est quaeque simili ratione desiderant? Cur enim flammas quidem sursum levitas vehit, terras vero deorsum pondus deprimit, nisi quod haec singulis loca motionesque conveniunt? Porro autem quod cuique consentaneum est, id unumquodque conservat, sicuti ea quae sunt inimica corrumpunt. Iam vero quae dura sunt ut lapides,

in mountains, some in marshes and some on rocks, while others thrive on barren sands. If you tried to transplant any of them to other places, they would die. But nature gives to each what is appropriate for it and works hard to prevent their destruction as long as possible.

"And what about trees which, as it were, with their mouths buried in the ground, draw up nourishment from their roots and disperse this strength through their pith[24] and bark? And what about the fact that the softest part, as the pith is, is hidden away on the inside and protected on the outside by a certain strength of wood, so that the bark suffers the hardship and acts as a kind of guardian against the harshness of weather? And truly how diligent nature is in propagating everything by the multiplying of seeds! Who doesn't know that all of these things are like machines that endure not only for their own lifetimes but also from one generation to the next forever?

"And don't even those things that are believed to be inanimate in a similar way seek what is fitting for themselves?[25] For why else does lightness carry flames upward or weight force earth downward except that these places and movements are appropriate to them? Moreover, what is fitting for each thing is also what preserves it, just as what is unfitting destroys it. Indeed hard things like rocks cling

adhaerent tenacissime partibus suis et ne facile dissolvantur resistunt. Quae vero liquentia ut aer atque aqua, facile quidem dividentibus cedunt, sed cito in ea rursus a quibus sunt abscisa relabuntur, ignis vero omnem refugit sectionem.

"Neque nunc nos de voluntariis animae cognoscentis motibus, sed de naturali intentione tractamus, sicuti est quod acceptas escas sine cogitatione transigimus, quod in somno spiritum ducimus nescientes; nam ne in animalibus quidem manendi amor ex animae voluntatibus, verum ex naturae principiis venit. Nam saepe mortem cogentibus causis quam natura reformidat voluntas amplectitur, contraque illud quo solo mortalium rerum durat diuturnitas gignendi opus, quod natura semper appetit, interdum coercet voluntas. Adeo haec sui caritas non ex animali motione sed ex naturali intentione procedit. Dedit enim providentia creatis a se rebus hanc vel maximam manendi causam ut quoad possunt naturaliter manere desiderent; quare nihil est quod ullo modo queas dubitare cuncta quae sunt appetere naturaliter constantiam permanendi, devitare perniciem."

"Confiteor," inquam, "nunc me indubitato cernere quae dudum incerta videbantur."

tenaciously to their parts and fight back against being easily destroyed. On the other hand, things that are fluid like air and water yield easily to dividing forces, but the separated parts quickly flow back again into the unities they were before. Fire, however, rejects all division.

"Of course we're not here discussing voluntary motions of intelligent souls but instead natural exertions, as when we digest the food we've eaten without conscious thought or breathe at night without thinking about it. For not even in living creatures does a desire for survival come from the active will of the soul but instead from principles of nature. Indeed, when driven by compelling causes, the will embraces the death from which nature recoils. On the other hand, the will sometimes resists the act of procreation that nature always desires as the only way of ensuring that mortal creatures continue. So this love of self proceeds not from the motion of the soul but from the striving of nature. Providence indeed has given to all created things this most important tool of surviving, that by their nature they desire to endure as long as they are able. Therefore there is no reason you should in any way doubt that *everything* that exists naturally seeks to remain unchanged and avoid destruction."

"I confess," I said, "that I now have no doubt about these things that seemed uncertain to me before."

"Quod autem," inquit, "subsistere ac permanere petit, id unum esse desiderat; hoc enim sublato ne esse quidem cuiquam permanebit."

"Verum est," inquam.

"Omnia igitur," inquit, "unum desiderant."

"Consensi."

"Sed unum id ipsum monstravimus esse quod bonum."

"Ita quidem."

"Cuncta igitur bonum petunt, quod quidem ita describas licet: ipsum bonum esse quod desideretur ab omnibus."

"Nihil," inquam, "verius excogitari potest. Nam vel ad nihil unum cuncta referuntur et uno veluti vertice destituta sine rectore fluitabunt, aut si quid est ad quod universa festinent, id erit omnium summum bonorum."

Et illa: "Nimium," inquit, "o alumne laetor, ipsam enim mediae veritatis notam mente fixisti. Sed in hoc patuit tibi quod ignorare te paulo ante dicebas."

"Quid?" inquam.

"Quis esset," inquit, "rerum omnium finis. Is est enim profecto, quod desideratur ab omnibus,

"Now then," she said, "that which seeks to survive and endure, doesn't it desire to be one? For with this taken away not even existence will remain for anything."

"That is true," I said.

"Everything therefore," she said, "desires oneness."

"I agree."

"But haven't we shown that which is one is also the good?"

"Indeed we have."

"Therefore everything seeks the good, which you therefore describe as follows: The good itself is that which is desired by all things."

"Nothing more true," I said, "can be imagined. For either all things are unrelated to any unifying thing and devoid of oneness directing them as they drift about with no guide, or, if there is something toward which everything hastens, it will be the highest of all goods."

And she said, "I am so happy, my dear child, that you have fixed in your mind that very idea[26] that is at the center of this truth. But now it has become clear to you what just a little while ago you said you didn't know at all."

"What?" I said.

"That," she said, "which is the goal of all things, since it's abundantly clear that this goal is what is

quod quia bonum esse collegimus, oportet rerum omnium finem bonum esse fateamur."

Tum ego: "Platoni," inquam, "vehementer assentior, nam me horum iam secundo commemoras, primum quod memoriam corporea contagione, dehinc cum maeroris mole pressus amisi."

Tum illa: "Si priora," inquit, "concessa respicias, ne illud quidem longius aberit quin recorderis quod te dudum nescire confessus es."

"Quid?" inquam.

"Quibus," ait illa, "gubernaculis mundus regatur."

"Memini," inquam, "me inscitiam meam fuisse confessum, sed quid afferas, licet iam prospiciam, planius tamen ex te audire desidero."

"Mundum," inquit, "hunc deo regi paulo ante minime dubitandum putabas."

"Ne nunc quidem arbitror," inquam, "nec umquam dubitandum putabo quibusque in hoc rationibus accedam breviter exponam.

"Mundus hic ex tam diversis contrariisque partibus in unam formam minime convenisset, nisi unus

desired by all things. And since we have agreed that this goal is the good, we must therefore confess that the goal desired by all things is the good."

The Goodness of God Rules the World

Then I said: "I strongly agree with Plato, for you're now reminding me of these things for the second time. The first time was when I lost my memory through contamination of the body,[27] then the second was when I was oppressed by the weight of grief."

Then she spoke: "So, if you look back on the principles we agreed to earlier, you'll not be far from remembering what you said you didn't know."

"What is that?" I asked.

"By what manner," she said, "the world is governed."

"I remember," I said, "that I confessed my ignorance, but although I can see dimly what you're going to say, I still desire for you to make it clearer."

"A little while ago," she said, "you had no doubt that this world is ruled by God."

"Not now," I said, "nor ever will I think that this can be doubted. I'll give you the reasons why I have come to this conclusion.

"This world could scarcely have come together into one form from such diverse and opposite parts

esset qui tam diversa coniungeret. Coniuncta vero naturarum ipsa diversitas invicem discors dissociaret atque divelleret, nisi unus esset qui quod nexuit contineret. Non tam vero certus naturae ordo procederet nec tam dispositos motus locis, temporibus, efficientia, spatiis, qualitatibus explicarent, nisi unus esset qui has mutationum varietates manens ipse disponeret. Hoc quidquid est quo condita manent atque agitantur, usitato cunctis vocabulo deum nomino."

Tum illa: "Cum haec," inquit, "ita sentias, parvam mihi restare operam puto ut felicitatis compos patriam sospes revisas. Sed quae proposuimus intueamur. Nonne in beatitudine sufficientiam numeravimus deumque beatitudinem ipsam esse consensimus?"

"Ita quidem."

"Et ad mundum igitur," inquit, "regendum nullis extrinsecus adminiculis indigebit; alioquin si quo egeat, plenam sufficientiam non habebit."

"Id," inquam, "ita est necessarium."

"Per se igitur solum cuncta disponit."

"Negari," inquam, "nequit."

unless there was someone who joined together such different things. Moreover, this conjoined and discordant diversity of natures would have shattered and fallen apart unless there was someone who continued to hold it all together. Also there couldn't be any fixed order of nature moving forward nor could the different parts arrange such orderly movements of place, time, effect, distance, and quality unless there was someone who, while remaining unchanged himself, arranged these variety of changes. This one thing by which created things are established and remain—using the word commonly used by everyone—I call God."

Then she said: "Since this is what you believe, I think there remains only a little work for me to do to restore you safe and sound to your homeland, ready to embrace happiness. But let's look closely at the conclusions we've proposed. Haven't we shown that self-sufficiency is included within true happiness and that God himself is true happiness?"

"Indeed we have."

"And therefore," she said, "to govern the world he will need no external means of support. For if he lacked something, he wouldn't have complete sufficiency."

"That," I said, "is necessarily so."

"He therefore arranges all things by himself?"

"I am not able," I said, "to deny it."

"Atqui deus ipsum bonum esse monstratus est."

"Memini," inquam.

"Per bonum igitur cuncta disponit, si quidem per se regit omnia quem bonum esse consensimus et hic est veluti quidam clavus atque gubernaculum quo mundana machina stabilis atque incorrupta servatur."

"Vehementer assentior," inquam, "et id te paulo ante dicturam tenui licet suspicione prospexi."

"Credo," inquit, "iam enim ut arbitror vigilantius ad cernenda vera oculos deducis. Sed quod dicam non minus ad contuendum patet."

"Quid?" inquam.

"Cum deus," inquit, "omnia bonitatis clavo gubernare iure credatur eademque omnia sicuti docui ad bonum naturali intentione festinent, num dubitari potest quin voluntaria regantur seque ad disponentis nutum veluti convenientia contemperataque rectori sponte convertant?"

"Ita," inquam, "necesse est; nec beatum regimen esse videretur, si quidem detrectantium iugum foret, non obtemperantium salus."

"Nihil est igitur quod naturam servans deo contrarie conetur."

"And God has been shown to be the good itself."

"I remember," I said.

"So through the good he arranges all things, if indeed he himself who we agree is the good rules all things by means of himself, like a tiller and rudder by which the machine of the world is preserved stable and unharmed."

"I absolutely agree," I said, "and this is why a little while ago I said I saw, though only in a dim way, what you were going to say."

"I believe you," she said, "for I think you're now directing your gaze more vigilantly toward the truth. But what I'm about to say now will be no less obvious for you to see."

"What is that?" I asked.

"Since God," she said, "is rightly believed to steer all things with the rudder of goodness and since all these things, as I taught you, hurry toward the good by natural intention, surely it can't be doubted that these things are ruled voluntarily and, possessing a free will, turn themselves agreeably and gladly toward the one who rules them?"

"That," I said, "would be necessary. His governance would not seem truly happy if indeed it were a yoke for those who rejected it and not the well-being for those who obey."

"So there is nothing that while preserving its own nature tries to act contrary to God."

"Nihil," inquam.

"Quod si conetur," ait, "num tandem proficiet quidquam adversus eum quem iure beatitudinis potentissimum esse concessimus?"

"Prorsus," inquam, "nihil valeret."

"Non est igitur aliquid quod summo huic bono vel velit vel possit obsistere."

"Non," inquam, "arbitror."

"Est igitur summum," inquit, "bonum quod regit cuncta fortiter suaviterque disponit."

Tum ego: "Quam," inquam, "me non modo ea quae conclusa est summa rationum, verum multo magis haec ipsa quibus uteris verba delectant, ut tandem aliquando stultitiam magna lacerantem sui pudeat."

"Accepisti," inquit, "in fabulis lacessentes caelum Gigantas; sed illos quoque, uti condignum fuit, benigna fortitudo disposuit. Sed visne rationes ipsas invicem collidamus? Forsitan ex huiusmodi conflictatione pulchra quaedam veritatis scintilla dissiliat."

"Tuo," inquam, "arbitratu."

"Deum," inquit, "esse omnium potentem nemo dubitaverit?"

"Qui quidem," inquam, "mente consistat, nullus prorsus ambigat."

"Nothing," I said.

"And if something tried," she said, "would it have any success against the one whom we have rightly agreed is most powerful in true happiness?"

"It would," I said, "certainly fail."

"Therefore there is nothing that wishes or is able to oppose this highest good."

"I don't think so," I said.

"And so," she said, "it's the highest good that rules all firmly and arranges everything sweetly."[28]

Then I said: "How delightful are not only the conclusions you reach in the summit of your arguments, but even more so the very words you use, so that the foolishness tearing apart great things is ashamed of itself."

"Now," she said, "you've heard in stories of giants attacking the heavens. But those creatures also, as was proper, were put in their place by kindly force.[29] But would you like for us to smash our arguments against each other, so that perhaps from striking them together some beautiful spark of truth might fly out?"

"As you wish," I said.

"Then does anyone," she asked, "doubt that God has power over everything?"

"If they are in their right mind," I said, "no one can doubt this."

"Qui vero est," inquit, "omnium potens, nihil est quod ille non possit."

"Nihil," inquam.

"Num igitur deus facere malum potest?"

"Minime," inquam.

"Malum igitur," inquit, "nihil est, cum id facere ille non possit, qui nihil non potest."

"Ludisne," inquam, "me inextricabilem labyrinthum rationibus texens, quae nunc quidem qua egrediaris introeas, nunc vero quo introieris egrediare, an mirabilem quendam divinae simplicitatis orbem complicas? Etenim paulo ante beatitudine incipiens eam summum bonum esse dicebas quam in summo deo sitam loquebare. Ipsum quoque deum summum esse bonum plenamque beatitudinem disserebas; ex quo neminem beatum fore nisi qui pariter deus esset quasi munusculum dabas. Rursus ipsam boni formam dei ac beatitudinis loquebaris esse substantiam ipsumque unum id ipsum esse bonum docebas quod ab omni rerum natura peteretur. Deum quoque bonitatis gubernaculis universitatem regere disputabas volentiaque cuncta parere nec ullam mali esse naturam. Atque haec nullis extrinsecus sumptis sed ex altero altero fidem trahente insitis domesticisque probationibus explicabas."

"Now," she said, "for the one who has all power, there is nothing he cannot do."

"Nothing," I said.

"But God cannot do evil, can he?"

"Not at all," I said.

"Therefore," she said, "evil is nothing, for God is not able to do it and there is nothing he cannot do."[30]

"Are you toying with me" I asked, "by weaving an impossible labyrinth of logic? For now you're entering by the way you exited, then leaving by the way you entered. Or are you joining together the ends of some wonderful circle of divine simplicity? For just a little while ago you started with true happiness and said it was the highest good and that it was located in God, who is the highest. Then you explained how God himself being the highest good is therefore complete and true happiness. From this you gave me a little gift, as it were, saying that no one is able to be truly happy unless they also became like God. Then you taught me that the very essence of God is goodness and true happiness, and that oneness itself is the very substance of goodness that is naturally sought by all things. You also showed me that God directs the universe by rudders of goodness and that all things willingly obey him and that evil has no real nature. And you proved all these things with arguments not drawn from the

Tum illa: "Minime," inquit, "ludimus remque omnium maximam dei munere quem dudum deprecabamur exegimus. Ea est enim divinae forma substantiae ut neque in externa dilabatur nec in se externum aliquid ipsa suscipiat, sed, sicut de ea Parmenides ait:

> Πάντοθεν εὐκύκλου σφαίρης ἐναλίγκιον ὄγκω,

rerum orbem mobilem rotat, dum se immobilem ipsa conservat. Quod si rationes quoque non extra petitas sed intra rei quam tractabamus ambitum collocatas agitavimus, nihil est quod admirere, cum Platone sanciente didiceris cognatos de quibus loquuntur rebus oportere esse sermones."

outside but with inherent and internal proofs supporting each other."

Then she spoke: "We are in no way playing a game. For this conclusion that we've reached is the greatest fact of all and is a gift of God to whom we prayed just a little while ago. For the essence of the divine substance is that it doesn't disperse into external things nor does it take into itself anything external. But as Parmenides says:[31]

Like the body of a sphere, well-rounded on all sides

it turns the moving circle of the universe, while it keeps itself unmoving. But as if we have drawn on arguments not sought from outside but within the bounds of the topic we were discussing, there's no reason for you to be amazed, since you've learned under the authority of Plato that words should be related to the things spoken of."[32]

INCIPIT LIBER IV

Haec cum Philosophia dignitate vultus et oris gravitate servata leniter suaviterque cecinisset, tum ego nondum penitus insiti maeroris oblitus intentionem dicere adhuc aliquid parantis abrupi.

Et: "O," inquam, "veri praevia luminis quae usque adhuc tua fudit oratio, cum sui speculatione divina tum tuis rationibus invicta patuerunt, eaque mihi etsi ob iniuriae dolorem nuper oblita non tamen antehac prorsus ignorata dixisti. Sed ea ipsa est vel maxima nostri causa maeroris, quod, cum rerum bonus rector exsistat, vel esse omnino mala possint vel impunita praetereant; quod solum quanta dignum sit admiratione profecto consideras. At huic aliud maius adiungitur. Nam imperante florenteque nequitia virtus non solum praemiis caret, verum etiam sceleratorum pedibus subiecta calcatur et in locum facinorum supplicia luit. Quae fieri in regno scientis omnia, potentis omnia sed

BOOK 4
How Can Evil Go Unpunished?

Philosophy finished singing these verses softly and sweetly yet always with dignity in her appearance and seriousness in her voice. But I hadn't yet forgotten the sorrows that remained in my heart, so I interrupted her just as she was preparing to say something more.

"You," I said, "who lead us on toward the true light, the words you have poured forth up until now are both clearly divine when considered on their own and irrefutable according to your arguments. You spoke of things I had forgotten because of the sorrow caused by the wrongs done to me recently, but they were not completely unknown to me before. Here, however, is the greatest cause of my grief: Although the ruler of the universe is good, how can evil still exist and go unpunished? I beg you to consider just how astonishing this is. And another problem of even greater importance is connected to it: When evil flourishes and rules, how can virtue go unrewarded and even be thrown down and trampled under the feet of wicked men,

bona tantummodo volentis dei nemo satis potest nec admirari nec conqueri."

Tum illa: "Et esset," inquit, "infiniti stuporis omnibusque horribilius monstris, si, uti tu aestimas, in tanti velut patrisfamilias dispositissima domo vilia vasa colerentur, pretiosa sordescerent. Sed non ita est. Nam si ea quae paulo ante conclusa sunt inconvulsa servantur, ipso de cuius nunc regno loquimur auctore cognosces semper quidem potentes esse bonos, malos vero abiectos semper atque inbecillos nec sine poena umquam esse vitia nec sine praemio virtutes, bonis felicia, malis semper infortunata contingere multaque id genus quae sopitis querelis firma te soliditate corroborent. Et quoniam verae formam beatitudinis me dudum monstrante vidisti, quo etiam sita sit agnovisti, decursis omnibus quae praemittere necessarium puto, viam tibi quae te domum revehat ostendam. Pennas etiam tuae menti quibus se in altum tollere possit adfigam, ut perturbatione depulsa sospes in patriam meo ductu, mea semita, meis etiam vehiculis revertaris."

so that it is actually punished instead of vice? The fact that this happens in the kingdom of God, who knows all, has all power, and wills only the good, is beyond the ability of anyone to sufficiently be amazed at or complain about."

Then she spoke: "It would indeed be a matter of infinite wonder and more monstrous than all other horrors if, as you think, in the most well-ordered household of the master,[1] the worthless pots were cherished while the most precious were defiled. But this isn't so. For if the conclusions we reached before are preserved undamaged, then by the help of that same one of whose kingdom we are now speaking you will see that good people are always powerful, evil people are always cast down and weak, vices never go without punishment, virtues are always rewarded, happiness truly belongs to good people, misfortunes always happen to those who are evil, and many other things of this kind that will lay your complaints to rest and give you solid ground to stand on. And since you have seen the essence of true happiness from my previous demonstrations and you know where it lives, once we have looked at the things I think you need to know, then I will show you the way home. Indeed I will give your mind wings to fly up to the heights so that with all confusion dispelled you can return safely to the land

Tum ego: "Papae," inquam, "ut magna promittis! Nec dubito quin possis efficere; tu modo quem excitaveris ne moreris."

"Primum igitur," inquit, "bonis semper adesse potentiam, malos cunctis viribus esse desertos agnoscas licebit, quorum quidem alterum demonstratur ex altero. Nam cum bonum malumque contraria sint, si bonum potens esse constiterit, liquet inbecillitas mali; at si fragilitas clarescat mali, boni firmitas nota est. Sed uti nostrae sententiae fides abundantior sit, alterutro calle procedam nunc hinc nunc inde proposita confirmans.

"Duo sunt quibus omnis humanorum actuum constat effectus, voluntas scilicet ac potestas, quorum si alterutrum desit, nihil est quod explicari queat. Deficiente etenim voluntate ne aggreditur quidem quisque quod non vult; at si potestas absit, voluntas frustra sit. Quo fit ut si quem videas adipisci velle

of your father under my guidance, along my path, and by my conveyance."

The Wicked Have No Power

"Wonderful!" I said. "What great things you promise! And I have no doubt you can do them, but please don't delay now that you've excited me."

"First then," she said, "you should know that good people always possess power while bad people have no strength at all. The one is in fact proved from the other. For since good and evil are opposites, if it's established that goodness is powerful, then evil will necessarily be weak. And on the other hand, if the fragility of evil is obvious, then the strength of goodness is clear. And now, so that our opinion is even more trustworthy, I'm going to prove each of these statements in turn, first looking at one side and then the other.

"There are two things by which the outcome of every human action is achieved: will and power. If one of these is missing, then nothing is able to be done. For if the will is lacking, a person won't try to do what is not desired. But if the power to do something is lacking, then will isn't enough. So it is that if you see someone wanting to gain something they're

quod minime adipiscatur, huic obtinendi quod voluerit defuisse valentiam dubitare non possis."

"Perspicuum est," inquam, "nec ullo modo negari potest."

"Quem vero effecisse quod voluerit videas, num etiam potuisse dubitabis?"

"Minime."

"Quod vero quisque potest, in eo validus, quod vero non potest, in hoc imbecillis esse censendus est."

"Fateor," inquam.

"Meministine igitur," inquit, "superioribus rationibus esse collectum intentionem omnem voluntatis humanae quae diversis studiis agitur ad beatitudinem festinare?"

"Memini," inquam, "illud quoque esse demonstratum."

"Num recordaris beatitudinem ipsum esse bonum eoque modo, cum beatitudo petitur, ab omnibus desiderari bonum?"

"Minime," inquam "recordor, quoniam id memoriae fixum teneo."

"Omnes igitur homines boni pariter ac mali indiscreta intentione ad bonum pervenire nituntur?"

"Ita," inquam, "consequens est."

not obtaining, then you know that they don't have the power to obtain it."

"This is clear," I said, "and cannot in any way be denied."

"And when you see someone who has obtained what they desired, do you doubt they had the power to do it?"

"Not at all."

"So each person should be thought powerful regarding that which they can do, and weak in that which they cannot do."

"I admit that," I said.

"Now do you remember," she asked, "that in our previous arguments we concluded that the whole effort of human will, although pursued by many different paths, directs itself eagerly toward true happiness?"

"I remember," I said, "that this has been demonstrated."

"And you remember, don't you, that true happiness is goodness itself, and that when true happiness is sought, it's actually goodness that is longed for by everyone?"

"I don't have to recall it at all," I said, "since I hold it firmly fixed in my mind."

"So all humans, good and bad alike, strive to reach goodness whatever their intention?"

"Yes," I said, "that follows."

"Sed certum est adeptione boni bonos fieri."

"Certum."

"Adipiscuntur igitur boni quod appetunt?"

"Sic videtur."

"Mali vero si adipiscerentur quod appetunt bonum, mali esse non possent."

"Ita est."

"Cum igitur utrique bonum petant, sed hi quidem adipiscantur, illi vero minime, num dubium est bonos quidem potentes esse, qui vero mali sunt imbecillos?"

"Quisquis," inquam, "dubitat, nec rerum naturam nec consequentiam potest considerare rationum."

"Rursus," inquit, "si duo sint quibus idem secundum naturam propositum sit eorumque unus naturali officio id ipsum agat atque perficiat, alter vero naturale illud officium minime administrare queat, alio vero modo quam naturae convenit non quidem impleat propositum suum sed imitetur implentem, quemnam horum valentiorem esse decernis?"

"Etsi coniecto," inquam, "quid velis, planius tamen audire desidero."

"Ambulandi," inquit, "motum secundum naturam esse hominibus num negabis?"

"But it's certain that people become good by obtaining goodness."

"It is certain."

"So therefore good people have obtained what they sought?"

"So it seems."

"And if evil people obtained what they seek, which is goodness, then they couldn't be evil."

"That's true."

"So both groups seek goodness, but the former secure it while the latter don't. So can there be any doubt that good people are powerful, but evil people are weak?"

"Whoever doubts this," I said, "isn't looking clearly either at the way the world works or at the rational consequences of our argument."

"Again," she said, "if there are two people who are given the same natural task and one of them performs it and completes it according to his natural abilities while the other is not able at all to do the job, but uses some other method contrary to his nature and does not complete the task but only imitates the one who accomplished it—which of these would you say has more power?"

"Even if I could guess," I said, "what answer you want, I would rather hear it from you plainly."

"Would you deny," she then asked, "that the motion of walking is natural for humans?"

"Minime," inquam.

"Eiusque rei pedum officium esse naturale num dubitas?"

"Ne hoc quidem," inquam.

"Si quis igitur pedibus incedere valens ambulet aliusque cui hoc naturale pedum desit officium, manibus nitens ambulare conetur, quis horum iure valentior existimari potest?"

"Contexe," inquam, "cetera; nam quin naturalis officii potens eo qui idem nequeat valentior sit, nullus ambigat."

"Sed summum bonum, quod aeque malis bonisque propositum, boni quidem naturali officio virtutum petunt, mali vero variam per cupiditatem, quod adipiscendi boni naturale officium non est, idem ipsum conantur adipisci. An tu aliter existimas?"

"Minime," inquam, "nam etiam quod est consequens patet. Ex his enim quae concesserim, bonos quidem potentes, malos vero esse necesse est imbecillos."

"Recte," inquit, "praecurris idque, uti medici sperare solent, indicium est erectae iam resistentisque naturae. Sed quoniam te ad intellegendum promptissimum esse conspicio, crebras coacervabo rationes.

"Not at all," I said.

"Do you doubt that performing that action is the natural function of feet?"

"I don't doubt that either," I said.

"So if someone who is able walks on his feet while another who lacks this natural use of his feet tries to walk relying on his hands, which of these two would you rightly say is stronger?"

"You can move on to your other arguments," I said, "for no one can doubt that the person able to use a natural function is stronger than the one who can't."

"Well then, the highest good sought by good and evil people alike, this good people seek by the natural functioning of their virtues, but evil people seek it through a variety of desires that are not a natural way for obtaining goodness. Or do you think otherwise?"

"Not at all," I said, "for it's obvious what the consequences are. From the points I have granted, it must be the case that good people are powerful, while evil people are by necessity weak."

"You're running ahead of me," she said, "and wonderfully so, for this is what a physician hopes for and is a sign of an alert and revived patient. But since I see that you're very eager to learn, I'll pile on the arguments swiftly.

"Vide enim quanta vitiosorum hominum pateat infirmitas qui ne ad hoc quidem pervenire queunt ad quod eos naturalis ducit ac paene compellit intentio. Et quid si hoc tam magno ac paene invicto praeeuntis naturae desererentur auxilio? Considera vero quanta sceleratos homines habeat impotentia. Neque enim levia aut ludicra praemia petunt, quae consequi atque obtinere non possunt, sed circa ipsam rerum summam verticemque deficiunt nec in eo miseris contingit effectus quod solum dies noctesque moliuntur; in qua re bonorum vires eminent.

"Sicut enim eum qui pedibus incedens ad eum locum usque pervenire potuisset, quo nihil ulterius pervium iaceret incessui, ambulandi potentissimum esse censeres, ita eum qui expetendorum finem quo nihil ultra est apprehendit, potentissimum necesse est iudices.

"Ex quo fit quod huic obiacet, ut idem scelesti, idem viribus omnibus videantur esse deserti. Cur enim relicta virtute vitia sectantur? Inscitiane bonorum? Sed quid enervatius ignorantiae caecitate? An sectanda noverunt, sed transversos eos libido praecipitat? Sic quoque intemperantia fragiles qui obluctari vitio nequeunt. An scientes volentesque bonum deserunt, ad vitia deflectunt? Sed hoc modo

"Just look at how great the weakness is of evil people who aren't even able to reach those goals toward which their natural inclinations draw and almost compel them. And what would happen if they were deserted by even this great and almost invincible help of nature leading their way? And consider the great powerlessness that holds wicked people. For the rewards they're seeking but cannot acquire or possess are not some small or trivial things.[2] The quest in which they fail is for the very height and summit of things. In their misery they can't achieve the only thing they strive so hard for day and night. It's in this same matter that the strength of good people shines forth.

"Just in the same way that you would judge most powerful a walking man who was able to reach on foot a place where he could go no farther, so too would you judge most powerful someone who achieves the end of all things desirable beyond which there is nothing else.

"The opposite is also true, that the same people who are wicked would also seem to be lacking in all power. For why indeed do they abandon virtue and follow after vice? Because they don't know what things are good? But then what greater weakness could there be than the blindness of ignorance? Or do they know what they should pursue, but their desires turn them sideways? But in this condition

non solum potentes esse sed omnino esse desinunt. Nam qui communem omnium quae sunt finem relinquunt, pariter quoque esse desistunt.

"Quod quidem cuipiam mirum forte videatur, ut malos, qui plures hominum sunt, eosdem non esse dicamus; sed ita sese res habet. Nam qui mali sunt eos malos esse non abnuo; sed eosdem esse pure atque simpliciter nego. Nam uti cadaver hominem mortuum dixeris, simpliciter vero hominem appellare non possis, ita vitiosos malos quidem esse concesserim, sed esse absolute nequeam confiteri. Est enim quod ordinem retinet servatque naturam; quod vero ab hac deficit, esse etiam, quod in sua natura situm est, derelinquit.

"'Sed possunt,' inquies, 'mali.' Ne ego quidem negaverim, sed haec eorum potentia non a viribus sed ab imbecillitate descendit. Possunt enim mala quae minime valerent, si in bonorum efficientia manere potuissent. Quae possibilitas eos evidentius nihil posse demonstrat. Nam si, uti paulo ante collegimus, malum nihil est, cum mala tantummodo possint, nihil posse improbos liquet."

they are also weak because they lack control to fight against vice. Or perhaps they knowingly and willingly forsake goodness and turn aside to vice? But if they do this, not only do they have no power, but they cease to exist. For in doing so they leave aside the common goal of everyone, thus they stop existing at all.

"Now it may seem a strange thing when we say that evil people, who are the majority of humanity, don't exist—but this is exactly what I mean. For while I don't deny that evil people are evil, I do deny that they exist in a real and essential sense. For just as you can call a corpse a dead human being, you cannot simply call it a human being. In the same way I would agree that there are evil and vile people, but I cannot admit that they exist in an absolute sense. For that which exists keeps its order and preserves its nature. But whatever falls away from this nature also abandons its existence, which is dependent on its nature.

"'But,' you will say, 'evil people have power.' Indeed, I don't deny this, but their power comes not from their strength but from their weakness. For all they can do is evil, which they would have been unable to do at all if they had been able to continue doing good things. And this so-called power they have only shows that they have no power. For if, as we agreed a little while ago, evil is nothing, then

"Perspicuum est."

"Atque ut intellegas quaenam sit huius potentiae vis, summo bono nihil potentius esse paulo ante definivimus."

"Ita est," inquam.

"Sed idem," inquit, "facere malum nequit."

"Minime."

"Est igitur," inquit, "aliquis qui omnia posse homines putet?"

"Nisi quis insaniat, nemo."

"Atqui idem possunt mala."

"Utinam quidem," inquam, "non possent."

"Cum igitur bonorum tantummodo potens possit omnia, non vero queant omnia potentes etiam malorum, eosdem qui mala possunt minus posse manifestum est. Huc accedit quod omnem potentiam inter expetenda numerandam omniaque expetenda referri ad bonum velut ad quoddam naturae suae cacumen ostendimus. Sed patrandi sceleris possibilitas referri ad bonum non potest; expetenda igitur non est. Atqui omnis potentia expetenda est; liquet igitur malorum possibilitatem non esse potentiam. Ex quibus omnibus bonorum quidem potentia,

in being able only to do evil they are in fact able to do nothing."

"That is obvious."

"And so you can understand what the nature of their power is, remember a little while ago we said that there is nothing more powerful than the highest good."

"This is true," I said.

"But this same highest good," she said, "cannot do evil."

"Not at all."

"Is there anyone," she asked, "who thinks that humans can do all things?"

"Unless they are insane, no one."

"And yet people can do evil."

"Oh how I wish," I exclaimed, "that they could not!"

"Therefore, since the one who has the power to do all things can do only good things, while those who have the power to do evil things cannot do all things, it is clear that those who are able to do evil are less powerful. In addition we've shown that all power is to be included among those things that should be desired and that all desired things are related to goodness as to the summit of their nature. But it isn't possible that committing evil is related to goodness, and therefore is not something to be desired. Yet all power is to be desired, so it's clear

malorum vero minime dubitabilis apparet infirmitas veramque illam Platonis esse sententiam liquet solos quod desiderent facere posse sapientes, improbos vero exercere quidem quod libeat, quod vero desiderent explere non posse. Faciunt enim quaelibet, dum per ea quibus delectantur id bonum quod desiderant se adepturos putant; sed minime adipiscuntur, quoniam ad beatitudinem probra non veniunt.

"Videsne igitur quanto in caeno probra volvantur, qua probitas luce resplendeat? In quo perspicuum est numquam bonis praemia numquam sua sceleribus deesse supplicia. Rerum etenim quae geruntur illud propter quod unaquaeque res geritur, eiusdem rei praemium esse non iniuria videri potest, uti currendi in stadio propter quam curritur iacet praemium corona. Sed beatitudinem esse idem ipsum bonum propter quod omnia geruntur ostendimus. Est igitur humanis actibus ipsum bonum veluti praemium commune propositum. Atqui hoc a bonis non potest separari neque enim bonus ultra

that the power to do evil is not a real power. From considering all of this it is obvious that good people have power and evil people are undoubtedly weak. So the opinion of Plato is true that only wise people have the power to do what they desire, but foolish people, though they keep very busy at whatever pleases them, are unable to achieve what they desire.[3] For evil people do whatever they like thinking that the things they enjoy will bring them what they desire. But they never get them since shameful deeds do not lead to true happiness.

Good People Are Like Gods, Bad People Are Like Beasts

"Do you see then in what filth wickedness wallows and with what light goodness shines? From all this it's obvious that rewards are never lacking for good people nor suitable punishments for the wicked. For any action that is performed, the particular reason for which it is undertaken can reasonably be seen as the reward for that action. For example, when someone runs a race in a stadium, a crown is set forth as the reward.[4] But we have shown that true happiness is a good in itself and the reason for which everything is done. Therefore the good itself is held forth, as it were, as the common reward for all

iure vocabitur qui careat bono; quare probos mores sua praemia non relinquunt. Quantumlibet igitur saeviant mali, sapienti tamen corona non decidet, non arescet. Neque enim probis animis proprium decus aliena decerpit improbitas.

"Quod si extrinsecus accepto laetaretur, poterat hoc vel alius quispiam vel ipse etiam qui contulisset auferre; sed quoniam id sua cuique probitas confert, tum suo praemio carebit, cum probus esse desierit. Postremo cum omne praemium idcirco appetatur quoniam bonum esse creditur, quis boni compotem praemii iudicet expertem? At cuius praemii? Omnium pulcherrimi maximique. Memento etenim corollarii illius quod paulo ante praecipuum dedi ac sic collige: cum ipsum bonum beatitudo sit, bonos omnes eo ipso quod boni sint fieri beatos liquet. Sed qui beati sint deos esse convenit. Est igitur praemium bonorum quod nullus deterat dies, nullius minuat potestas, nullius fuscet improbitas, deos fieri.

human actions. But this reward cannot be separated from good people—since no one is called good if they are lacking in goodness—on account of which upright conduct is never lacking in proper rewards. And so however much evil people may rage, the crown never falls from the head of the wise person nor does it wither away. And the wickedness of another person can never steal from righteous souls the glory that is theirs alone.

"If a person rejoices in a reward given by someone, that reward could still be taken away by another person or even by the person who gave it. But since it is one's own goodness that gives each good person a reward, you will only lack that reward when you cease to be good. Finally, since every reward is desired because it is believed to be good, who would judge a person who possesses goodness to be lacking in a reward? But what is this reward? Only the best and most beautiful thing of all. Remember the corollary I gave you a little while ago as a gift and consider this: Since true happiness is the good itself, it's clear that all good people—by the very fact that they are good—become truly happy. But we agreed that those who are truly happy are gods. So the reward of good people—a reward time cannot diminish, no one's power can lessen, and the wickedness of none can obscure—is to become gods.

“Quae cum ita sint, de malorum quoque inseparabili poena dubitare sapiens nequeat. Nam cum bonum malumque item poenae atque praemium adversa frontedissideant, quae in boni praemio videmus accedere eadem necesse est in mali poena contraria parte respondeant. Sicut igitur probis probitas ipsa fit praemium, ita improbis nequitia ipsa supplicium est. Iam vero quisquis afficitur poena, malo se affectum esse non dubitat. Si igitur sese ipsi aestimare velint, possuntne sibi supplicii expertes videri quos omnium malorum extrema nequitia non affecit modo verum etiam vehementer infecit?

“Vide autem ex adversa parte bonorum, quae improbos poena comitetur. Omne namque quod sit unum esse ipsumque unum bonum esse paulo ante didicisti, cui consequens est ut omne quod sit id etiam bonum esse videatur. Hoc igitur modo quidquid a bono deficit esse desistit; quo fit ut mali desinant esse quod fuerant, sed fuisse homines adhuc ipsa humani corporis reliqua species ostentat. Quare versi in malitiam humanam quoque amisere naturam.

"Since all of this is true for good people, no wise person is able to doubt that punishment is also inseparable from bad people. For just as good and evil, like punishment and reward, are opposites of each other,[5] what we see as a reward for good people must necessarily occur in the opposite way as punishment for bad people. Therefore goodness itself is the reward for good people, but wickedness is surely the punishment for the wicked. Now those who have been afflicted by punishment have no doubt that they have been struck by an evil thing. If therefore these people were willing to take the measure of their own condition, could they suppose themselves to have no punishment, since they are not only touched by the worst of all evils but disastrously infected?

"Now consider it from the opposite side of goodness and see what punishment is the constant companion of the wicked. A little while ago you learned that everything that truly exists is unified and that oneness itself is good. From this it follows that everything that has true existence appears to be good. In this same way whatever falls away from goodness ceases to exist. And so evil people cease to be the humans they once were. But the fact that they still have human bodies shows that they were once human. But because they turned to wickedness, they've lost their essential humanity as well.

"Sed cum ultra homines quemque provehere sola probitas possit, necesse est ut quos ab humana condicione deiecit, infra hominis meritum detrudat improbitas. Evenit igitur, ut quem transformatum vitiis videas hominem aestimare non possis. Avaritia fervet alienarum opum violentus ereptor? Lupi similem dixeris. Ferox atque inquies linguam litigiis exercet? Cani comparabis. Insidiator occultus subripuisse fraudibus gaudet? Vulpeculis exaequetur. Irae intemperans fremit? Leonis animum gestare credatur. Pavidus ac fugax non metuenda formidat? Cervis similis habeatur. Segnis ac stupidus torpit? Asinum vivit. Levis atque inconstans studia permutat? Nihil avibus differt. Foedis inmundisque libidinibus immergitur? Sordidae suis voluptate detinetur. Ita fit ut qui probitate deserta homo esse desierit, cum in divinam condicionem transire non possit, vertatur in beluam."

Tum ego: "Fateor," inquam, "nec iniuria dici video vitiosos, tametsi humani corporis speciem servent, in beluas tamen animorum qualitate mutari; sed

"Since only goodness can lift anyone up beyond the human, it's necessary that wickedness casts evil people down below the level of being considered human. So it happens that whoever you might see who has been transformed by wickedness is not able to be reckoned as human. Does some thief burn with desire for the wealth of others? You could say he's like a wolf. The wild and restless man always yapping his tongue in lawsuits? He's like a dog. The one lying in wait always glad to steal by deception? He's on the same level as a fox. Someone who rages and roars unable to control his anger? He has the spirit of a lion inside him. The timid man running away from things that shouldn't be feared? He's like a deer. Someone else is lazy and dull-witted? He lives the life of an ass. Another is fickle and always changing his goals? He's no different from the birds. Someone wallows in foul and unclean desires? He has the mind of a filthy sow. So whoever has abandoned righteousness and ceased to be a human being, since he cannot rise to a divine condition, is turned into a beast."

The Wicked Are Miserable

Then I said: "I'll admit that I see how wicked people are said to turn into beasts in the quality of their minds while still retaining the form of a human

quorum atrox scelerataque mens bonorum pernicie saevit, id ipsum eis licere noluissem."

"Nec licet," inquit, "uti convenienti monstrabitur loco. Sed tamen si id ipsum quod eis licere creditur auferatur, magna ex parte sceleratorum hominum poena relevetur. Etenim quod incredibile cuiquam forte videatur, infeliciores esse necesse est malos, cum cupita perfecerint, quam si ea quae cupiunt implere non possint. Nam si miserum est voluisse prava, potuisse miserius est, sine quo voluntatis miserae langueret effectus. Itaque cum sua singulis miseria sit, triplici infortunio necesse est urgeantur quos videas scelus velle, posse, perficere."

"Accedo," inquam, "sed uti hoc infortunio cito careant patrandi sceleris possibilitate deserti vehementer exopto."

"Carebunt," inquit, "ocius quam vel tu forsitan velis vel illi sese aestiment esse carituros. Neque enim est aliquid in tam brevibus vitae metis ita serum quod exspectare longum immortalis praesertim animus putet: quorum magna spes et excelsa facinorum machina repentino atque insperato saepe

body. But those savage and evil minds of theirs do act brutally in destroying good people. I wish they were not allowed to do this."

"But they aren't allowed," she said, "as I will show you in the proper place. But nonetheless, if this power believed to be allowed to them should be taken away, the punishment due these wicked people would largely be taken away. And as incredible as it may seem to some, wicked people are in fact more unhappy when they achieve what they desire than when they're not able to do the evil things they want. For if it brings a person misery to simply desire evil things, it's even more miserable to have the power to do them. Without this power, the effectiveness of evil fades away. Each of these three stages individually has its own misery, but it's a triple curse on those who first want to do evil, second are able to do it, and third actually carry the evil through to completion."

"I'll grant that," I said, "but I seriously wish these people would lose their power to do evil and so be freed from this punishment."[6]

"Oh, they will lose it," she said, "and perhaps sooner than you might wish or they think they will. For there is nothing in the span of human life, being as short as it is, that comes late for an immortal soul. The great hopes of evil people and all their lofty machinations are quickly and often suddenly

fine destruitur, quod quidem illis miseriae modum statuit. Nam si nequitia miseros facit, miserior sit necesse est diuturnior nequam; quos infelicissimos esse iudicarem, si non eorum malitiam saltem mors extrema finiret. Etenim si de pravitatis infortunio vera conclusimus, infinitam liquet esse miseriam quam esse constat aeternam."

Tum ego: "Mira quidem," inquam, "et concessu difficilis inlatio, sed his eam quae prius concessa sunt nimium convenire cognosco."

"Recte," inquit, "aestimas. Sed qui conclusioni accedere durum putat, aequum est vel falsum aliquid praecessisse demonstret vel collocationem propositionum non esse efficacem necessariae conclusionis ostendat; alioquin concessis praecedentibus nihil prorsus est quod de inlatione causetur. Nam hoc quoque quod dicam non minus mirum videatur, sed ex his quae sumpta sunt aeque est necessarium."

"Quidnam?" inquam.

"Feliciores," inquit, "esse improbos supplicia luentes quam si eos nulla iustitiae poena coerceat. Neque id nunc molior quod cuivis veniat in mentem, corrigi ultione pravos mores et ad rectum supplicii terrore deduci, ceteris quoque exemplum

destroyed by death. And that at least sets a limit to their wretchedness. For if wickedness makes people miserable, it's necessarily the case that the longer someone is wicked, the longer they are miserable. I would judge them to be unhappy without limit except that death at least sets a boundary to their wickedness. For if we have concluded correctly about the misery that comes to evil people, wickedness without limit would be eternal."

Then I spoke: "Your conclusion is strange indeed and difficult to admit, but I understand that it very much follows from the points we agreed on earlier."

"You judge rightly," she said. "For if someone thinks it hard to agree to a conclusion, they have to show either that some false premise preceded it or that the premises when added together don't produce a necessary conclusion. Otherwise there is no justified reason to dispute the conclusion reached if all the preceding premises have been agreed upon. Now this conclusion I'm about to present you will seem no less surprising but is equally necessary given the things we have already decided are true."

"What conclusion is that?" I asked.

"That wicked people," she said, "are happier when they are punished than if they escape the penalty required by justice. I'm not trying to build a case against a point that might come into anyone's mind, namely that evil ways are corrected by

esse culpanda fugiendi, sed alio quodam modo infeliciores esse improbos arbitror impunitos, tametsi nulla ratio correctionis, nullus respectus habeatur exempli."

"Et quis erit," inquam, "praeter hos alius modus?"

Et ilia: "Bonos," inquit, "esse felices, malos vero miseros nonne concessimus?"

"Ita est," inquam.

"Si igitur," inquit, "miseriae cuiuspiam bonum aliquid addatur, nonne felicior est eo cuius pura ac solitaria sine cuiusquam boni admixtione miseria est?"

"Sic," inquam, "videtur."

"Quid si eidem misero qui cunctis careat bonis, praeter ea quibus miser est malum aliud fuerit adnexum, nonne multo infelicior eo censendus est cuius infortunium boni participatione relevatur?"

"Quidni," inquam.

"Sed puniri improbos iustum, impunitos vero elabi iniquum esse manifestum est?"

"Quis id neget?"

"Sed ne illud quidem," ait, "quisquam negabit bonum esse omne quod iustum est contraque quod iniustum est malum."

retribution and led back to the right path by fear of punishment and that punishment is an example for other people that causes them to flee from doing evil in the first place. I'm thinking of a different way that wicked people are more unhappy when they go unpunished, even if we don't take into account correction or example."

"And what," I asked," will be the other way beyond these?"

Then she said, "Haven't we agreed that good people are happy and evil people are unhappy?"

"Yes we have," I said.

"And so," she said, "if some portion of goodness were added to someone who is unhappy, wouldn't that person be happier than someone who has nothing but pure misery with no good mixed in?"

"Yes," I said, "it seems so."

"Now, if to that unhappiness of a person who has no goodness at all were added some other evil besides the ones they had before, wouldn't they be considered much more unhappy than the wretched person who is relieved by some small bit of good?"

"Of course," I said.

"But it is clearly just for the wicked to be punished and unjust for them to escape punishment?"

"Who could deny it?"

"But there is no one," she said, "who would deny this either, namely that everything that is just

Liquere, respondi.

"Habent igitur improbi, cum puniuntur quidem boni aliquid adnexum poenam ipsam scilicet quae ratione iustitiae bona est, idemque cum supplicio carent, inest eis aliquid ulterius mali ipsa impunitas quam iniquitatis merito malum esse confessus es."

"Negare non possum."

"Multo igitur infeliciores improbi sunt iniusta impunitate donati quam iusta ultione puniti."

Tum ego: "Ista quidem consequentia sunt eis quae paulo ante conclusa sunt. Sed quaeso," inquam, "te, nullane animarum supplicia post defunctum morte corpus relinquis?"

"Et magna quidem," inquit, "quorum alia poenali acerbitate, alia vero purgatoria clementia exerceri puto. Sed nunc de his disserere consilium non est.

"Id vero hactenus egimus, ut quae indignissima tibi videbatur malorum potestas eam nullam esse cognosceres quosque impunitos querebare, videres numquam improbitatis suae carere suppliciis, licentiam quam cito finiri precabaris nec longam esse disceres infelicioremque fore, si diuturnior, infelicissimam

is good and, on the other hand, everything that is unjust is evil."

I responded that it was clear.

"The wicked, therefore, when they are punished, have some good added to them, namely the punishment itself that is good because it is just. And these same wicked people, when they go unpunished, have some further evil added to them, which is a lack of punishment, something you have agreed is evil by reason of its injustice."

"I cannot deny this."

"Therefore the wicked who are allowed an unjust lack of punishment are much more unhappy than those who are punished by just retribution."

Then I said: "These are indeed the logical consequences of what we concluded just a little while ago. But I must ask, do you allow for no punishment of souls after the body ends in death?"

"I do indeed," she said, "and I think some of those punishments are given in harsh retribution, while others are done with purifying kindness.[7] But now is not the time to consider these things.

"So far," she continued, "we've brought the discussion to the point that you've seen the power of evil people—which seemed so intolerable to you—is in fact nothing at all. You've also seen that those wicked people you complained went unpunished never in fact lack punishment for their evil deeds.

vero, si esset aeterna; post haec miseriores esse improbos iniusta impunitate dimissos quam iusta ultione punitos. Cui sententiae consequens est ut tum demum gravioribus suppliciis urgeantur, cum impuniti esse creduntur."

Tum ego: "Cum tuas," inquam, "rationes considero, nihil dici verius puto. At si ad hominum iudicia revertar, quis ille est cui haec non credenda modo sed saltem audienda videantur?"

"Ita est," inquit illa. "Nequeunt enim oculos tenebris assuetos ad lucem perspicuae veritatis attollere, similesque avibus sunt quarum intuitum nox inluminat dies caecat. Dum enim non rerum ordinem, sed suos intuentur affectus, vel licentiam vel impunitatem scelerum putant esse felicem. Vide autem quid aeterna lex sanciat. Melioribus animum conformaveris, nihil opus est iudice praemium deferente; tu te ipse excellentioribus addidisti. Studium ad peiora deflexeris, extra ne quaesieris ultorem. Tu te ipse in deteriora trusisti, veluti si vicibus sordidam humum caelumque respicias, cunctis extra cessantibus ipsa cernendi ratione nunc caeno nunc sideribus interesse videaris.

And you've learned that the freedom granted them to do evil, a freedom you prayed might end swiftly, is not truly long-lasting. In fact it would become more miserable the longer it did last and be most horrendous if it were eternal. Then after all this you learned that the wicked are actually more miserable if they escape with unjust impunity than if they are punished justly. The consequence of this conclusion is that evil people are oppressed by the heaviest punishments precisely when they are believed to go unpunished."

Then I spoke: "When I consider your arguments, nothing could seem more true to me. But if we look at the judgment of most people, is there anyone for whom your arguments would seem not just unworthy of belief but not even worth listening to?"

"You're right," she said, "for most people are not able lift their eyes, accustomed as they are to darkness, up to the light of truth. They're like birds who can see at night but are blinded in the daylight. As long as people don't look at the order of the universe but only at their own desires, they think that the ability to do evil deeds and go unpunished is a happy thing. But look at what eternal law has decreed. If you conform your mind to better things, you don't need a judge to give you a reward, for you have joined yourself to more excellent things. But if you turn your mind to baser things, you don't need to seek beyond yourself for punishment, for you have thrust

"At vulgus ista non respicit. Quid igitur? Hisne accedamus quos beluis similes esse monstravimus? Quid si quis amisso penitus visu ipsum etiam se habuisse oblivisceretur intuitum nihilque sibi ad humanam perfectionem deesse arbitraretur, num videntes eadem caeco putaremus? Nam ne illud quidem adquiescent quod aeque validis rationum nititur firmamentis: infeliciores eos esse qui faciant quam qui patiantur iniuriam."

"Vellem," inquam, "has ipsas audire rationes."

"Omnem," inquit, "improbum num supplicio dignum negas?"

"Minime."

"Infelices vero esse qui sint improbi multipliciter liquet."

"Ita," inquam.

"Qui igitur supplicio digni sunt miseros esse non dubitas?"

"Convenit," inquam.

yourself down among shameful things. It's just as if you looked in turn down at the squalid earth, then up at the sky: leaving aside all other things, you would seem to yourself by your perception to dwell now in the mud, now among the stars.

"But most people don't think about these things. What should we do then? Should we join those people we've proven are like beasts? But what if there was someone who had completely lost his sight and even forgotten that he could ever see at all, thinking there was nothing of human perfection lacking in him? Would we as seeing people believe the same thing as the blind man? For most people will not even concede the point, which rests on equally strong foundations, that those who commit injustice are more unhappy than those who suffer it."

"I would like," I said, "to hear these very arguments."

"Then would you deny," she asked, "that every wicked person is worthy of punishment?"

"Not at all."

"But it is obvious that wicked people are in many ways unhappy."

"It is," I said.

"So you wouldn't doubt that people worthy of punishment are miserable?"

"I would not," I said.

"Si igitur cognitor," ait, "resideres, cui supplicium inferendum putares, eine qui fecisset an qui pertulisset iniuriam?"

"Nec ambigo," inquam, "quin perpesso satisfacerem dolore facientis."

"Miserior igitur tibi iniuriae inlator quam acceptor esse videretur."

"Consequitur," inquam.

"Hinc igitur aliis de causis ea radice nitentibus, quod turpitudo suapte natura miseros faciat, apparet inlatam cuilibet iniuriam non accipientis sed inferentis esse miseriam."

<"Apparet," inquam.>[8]

"Atqui nunc," ait, "contra faciunt oratores. Pro his enim qui grave quid acerbumque perpessi sunt miserationem iudicum excitare conantur, cum magis admittentibus iustior miseratio debeatur; quos non ab iratis sed a propitiis potius miserantibusque accusatoribus ad iudicium veluti aegros ad medicum duci oportebat, ut culpae morbos supplicio resecarent. Quo pacto defensorum opera vel tota frigeret, vel si prodesse hominibus mallet, in accusationis habitum verteretur. Ipsi quoque improbi, si eis aliqua rimula virtutem relictam fas esset aspicere vitiorumque sordes poenarum cruciatibus se depondituros

"So if you were sitting as the judge," she said, "which of the two would you think should be punished—the one who harms or the one who suffers injury?"

"I have no doubt," I said, "that I would give satisfaction to the victim by punishing the one who did harm."

"Therefore the one who does injury would seem more wretched to you than the one who suffers it."

"That is logical," I said.

"And so it is for this reason and others resting on the same principle, that it is obvious shamelessness makes people miserable by its own nature and that an injury done to someone makes wretched not the one who receives the injury but the one who causes it."

"It is obvious," I said.

"And yet," she said, "prosecutors nowadays do just the opposite. They try to stir up the judges to have mercy on those who are victims of some serious and grievous crime. In fact a more just compassion is owed to those who commit crimes. It would be better if they were led to judgment not by angry prosecutors but rather by kindly and merciful ones, just like sick people brought to a physician, so that they might cut out the disease by their punishment. In this way the role of defense lawyers would fade away or, if they wanted to do some good for people, they could become prosecutors.

viderent, compensatione adipiscendae probitatis nec hos cruciatus esse ducerent defensorumque operam repudiarent ac se totos accusatoribus iudicibusque permitterent. Quo fit ut apud sapientes nullus prorsus odio locus relinquatur. Nam bonos quis nisi stultissimus oderit? Malos vero odisse ratione caret. Nam si, uti corporum languor, ita vitiositas quidam est quasi morbus animorum, cum aegros corpore minime dignos odio sed potius miseratione iudicemus, multo magis non insequendi sed miserandi sunt quorum mentes omni languore atrocior urget improbitas."

Hic ego: "Video," inquam, "quae sit vel felicitas vel miseria in ipsis proborum atque improborum meritis constituta. Sed in hac ipsa fortuna populari non nihil boni malive inesse perpendo. Neque enim

And the wicked themselves, if they were allowed to see through some small crack the virtue they left behind and perceive that they could lay aside the filth of their wickedness through the tortures of their punishments, they wouldn't think themselves suffering torments at all compared to the good they were acquiring. They would reject all efforts of their defense lawyers and instead give themselves over completely to the prosecutors and judges. And so it would be that among wise people there would be no place at all for hatred. For who would hate good people except utter fools? There would also be no reason to hate wicked people, for in the same way exhaustion is a disease of the body, wickedness is a disease of the mind. We judge those sick in their body worthy of compassion rather than hatred, so by how much more should wicked people be pitied rather than persecuted, since their minds are weakened by wickedness, something so much crueler than any bodily disease."

But Why Does God Allow Evil to Flourish?

Then I said: "I see the deserved happiness and misery that has been established for the deeds of the righteous and unrighteous. But as I consider things, there does seem to be some good as well as evil

sapientum quisquam exul inops ignominiosusque esse malit, potius quam pollens opibus, honore reverendus, potentia validus, in sua permanens urbe florere. Sic enim clarius testatiusque sapientiae tractatur officium, cum in contingentes populos regentium quodam modo beatitudo transfunditur, cum praesertim carcer, nex[9] ceteraque legalium tormenta poenarum perniciosis potius civibus propter quos etiam constituta sunt debeantur. Cur haec igitur versa vice mutentur scelerumque supplicia bonos premant, praemia virtutum mali rapiant, vehementer admiror, quaeque tam iniustae confusionis ratio videatur ex te scire desidero. Minus etenim mirarer, si misceri omnia fortuitis casibus crederem. Nunc stuporem meum deus rector exaggerat. Qui cum saepe bonis iucunda, malis aspera contraque bonis dura tribuat, malis optata concedat, nisi causa deprehenditur, quid est quod a fortuitis casibus differre videatur?"

in the common opinion about fortune. After all, there isn't any wise person who would prefer to be a poor and disgraced exile rather than be secure in riches, honored for position, strong in power, and flourishing at home in one's own city. For in this way the proper use of wisdom is carried out in a more visible and notable way, so that the true happiness of those ruling flows down in some way to the common people, especially when prison, execution, and other punishing torments of the law are reserved for the truly wicked citizens for whom they were established. And so I am utterly amazed that these things have in reality been reversed so that punishments for crimes overwhelm good people while evil people seize the rewards due to virtue. I would love to learn from you what the reason is for what seems to be such unjust confusion. I would be less amazed if I believed everything happened by random chance, but having God at the helm of the universe makes my astonishment all the greater. For while he often grants blessings to good people and bitter punishments to the wicked, he also lays harshness on good people and makes the dreams of evil people come true. Unless the reason for this can be discovered, how does his ordered universe differ from random chance?"

"Nec mirum," inquit, "si quid ordinis ignorata ratione temerarium confusumque credatur. Sed tu quamvis causam tantae dispositionis ignores, tamen quoniam bonus mundum rector temperat, recte fieri cuncta ne dubites."

"Ita est," inquam; "sed cum tui muneris sit latentium rerum causas evolvere velatasque caligine explicare rationes, quaeso uti quae hinc decernas, quoniam hoc me miraculum maxime perturbat, edisseras."

Tum illa paulisper arridens: "Ad rem me," inquit, "omnium quaesitu maximam vocas, cui vix exhausti quicquam satis sit. Talis namque materia est ut una dubitatione succisa innumerabiles aliae velut hydrae capita succrescant, nec ullus fuerit modus, nisi quis eas vivacissimo mentis igne coerceat. In hac enim de providentiae simplicitate, de fati serie, de repentinis casibus, de cognitione ac praedestinatione divina, de arbitrii libertate quaeri solet, quae quanti oneris sint ipse perpendis. Sed quoniam haec quoque te nosse quaedam medicinae tuae portio est, quamquam angusto limite temporis saepti tamen aliquid delibare conabimur. Quod si te musici

"It's not amazing," she said, "that something is believed to be random and confused if the reason behind it is unknown. But although you don't know the cause of this great arrangement, please don't doubt that a good ruler governs it all and that everything is done rightly."

Fate and the Providence of God

"Yes," I said, "but since it's your task to reveal the causes of hidden things and to unfold their reasons clouded in darkness, I beseech you to explain the conclusions you've drawn, for this thing beyond my understanding disturbs me greatly."

Then she spoke, smiling a little: "You're calling on me to discuss one of the greatest of questions, to which there is scarcely any sufficient answer. It's the kind of problem that when you've cut away one doubt, countless others spring up, like the heads of a hydra.[10] And there is no limit to these doubts unless you stop them with the most lively fire of the mind. For on this one matter hangs the weightiest problems: the singleness of providence, the chain of fate, the randomness of chance, the knowledge and predestination of God, and finally the freedom of the will. But since it is part of your medicine to understand these things, even though our time is

carminis oblectamenta delectant, hanc oportet paulisper differas voluptatem, dum nexas sibi ordine contexo rationes."

"Ut libet," inquam.

Tunc velut ab alio orsa principio ita disseruit: "Omnium generatio rerum cunctusque mutabilium naturarum progressus et quidquid aliquo movetur modo, causas, ordinem, formas ex divinae mentis stabilitate sortitur. Haec in suae simplicitatis arce composita multiplicem rebus regendis modum statuit. Qui modus cum in ipsa divinae intellegentiae puritate conspicitur, providentia nominatur; cum vero ad ea quae movet atque disponit refertur, fatum a veteribus appellatum est. Quae diversa esse facile liquebit, si quis utriusque vim mente conspexerit. Nam providentia est ipsa illa divina ratio in summo omnium principe constituta quae cuncta disponit; fatum vero inhaerens rebus mobilibus dispositio per quam providentia suis quaeque nectit ordinibus. Providentia namque cuncta pariter quamvis diversa quamvis infinita complectitur; fatum vero singula digerit in motum locis formis ac temporibus distributa, ut haec temporalis ordinis explicatio in divinae mentis adunata prospectum providentia sit,

limited, we'll try to have some discussion of them. If it's the delight of music and song that please you, you'll have to postpone that pleasure for a while until I weave together my arguments in due order."[11]

"As you please," I said.

Then as if beginning again from a new starting point she spoke: "The generation of all things and the whole progress of changeable natures and whatever is set in motion by whatever means—all these are given their causes, order, and forms from the stability of the divine mind. That mind, firmly established in the citadel of its own simplicity, has created the multifold manner by which all things are governed. When this manner is contemplated in the purity of the divine intelligence, it is called *providence*. But when it is related to those things it moves and arranges, it was called by the ancients *fate*. It's easy for someone to see that these are two different things if each is considered carefully in one's mind. For providence is the divine reason itself, established by the highest ruler of all things, who arranges all things. But fate is the disposition inherent in all things in motion, through which providence binds things in their proper order. Providence embraces all things equally even though they are diverse and infinite. Fate sets in motion individual things that are distributed in places, forms, and times. So the unfolding of the order of things in all time, unified

eadem vero adunatio digesta atque explicata temporibus fatum vocetur.

"Quae licet diversa sint, alterum tamen pendet ex altero. Ordo namque fatalis ex providentiae simplicitate procedit. Sicut enim artifex faciendae rei formam mente praecipiens movet operis effectum, et quod simpliciter praesentarieque prospexerat, per temporales ordines ducit, ita deus providentia quidem singulariter stabiliterque facienda disponit, fato vero haec ipsa quae disposuit multipliciter ac temporaliter administrat. Sive igitur famulantibus quibusdam providentiae divinis spiritibus fatum exercetur seu anima seu tota inserviente natura seu caelestibus siderum motibus seu angelica virtute seu daemonum varia sollertia seu aliquibus horum seu omnibus fatalis series texitur, illud certe manifestum est immobilem simplicemque gerendarum formam rerum esse providentiam, fatum vero eorum quae divina simplicitas gerenda disposuit mobilem nexum atque ordinem temporalem.

"Quo fit ut omnia quae fato subsunt providentiae quoque subiecta sint cui ipsum etiam subiacet fatum, quaedam vero quae sub providentia locata sunt fati

by the foresight of the divine mind, is providence. But the same unity when set out and unfolded in specific times is called fate.

"Now although these two things are different, still one depends on the other. The order of fate proceeds from the simplicity of providence. For a craftsman first conceives in his mind the form of a thing to be made, then in orderly stages of time sets in motion the creation of the work that he has previously envisioned in a simple and single moment. So too God by providence carries out what is to be done in a simple and timeless way, but by fate he manages these things in a diverse and temporal way. Now whether fate is driven by certain divine spirits acting as servants of providence or by soul[12] or by the service of all of nature or by the motion of stars in the heavens or the power of angels or by the varied skills of demons or by any or all of these things, it is clear that providence is the unmoving and simple form of things carried out, while fate is the weaving together in motion and ordering of time that divine simplicity has arranged to be carried out.[13]

"And so it is that all things subject to fate are also subject to providence, to which fate itself is subordinate. But there are certain things inferior to providence that are superior to the course of fate. These are things that are fixed unmoving next to the

seriem superent. Ea vero sunt quae primae propinqua divinitati stabiliter fixa fatalis ordinem mobilitatis execedunt. Nam ut orbium circa eundem cardinem sese vertentium qui est intimus ad simplicitatem medietatis accedit ceterorumque extra locatorum veluti cardo quidam circa quem versentur exsistit, extimus vero maiore ambitu rotatus quanto a puncti media individuitate discedit tanto amplioribus spatiis explicatur, si quid vero illi se medio conectat et societ, in simplicitatem cogitur diffundique ac diffluere cessat, simili ratione quod longius a prima mente discedit maioribus fati nexibus implicatur ac tanto aliquid fato liberum est quanto illum rerum cardinem vicinius petit. Quod si supernae mentis haeserit firmitati, motu carens fati quoque supergreditur necessitatem. Igitur uti est ad intellectum ratiocinatio, ad id quod est id quod gignitur, ad aeternitatem tempus, ad punctum medium circulus, ita est fati series mobilis ad providentiae stabilem simplicitatem.

"Ea series caelum ac sidera movet, elementa in se invicem temperat et alterna commutatione transformat; eadem nascentia occidentiaque omnia per similes fetuum seminumque renovat progressus.

supreme divinity and are beyond the ordering of movable fate. For just as when a number of circles turn around the same center point, the one that lies closest to the center approaches the simplicity of the middle, since all the other circles that lie outside of it turn around it as a kind of center point. But the outermost circle, turning as it is in a greater circumference, is separated from the unmoving center more and more the farther it is removed from that center. But if something were able to join and bind itself to the center, it is forced into simplicity and ceases to disperse and diffuse itself. Likewise that which is separated farthest from the first mind is entangled in tighter nets of fate—for a thing is freer from fate the more closely it seeks the center point of things. And if something can cling tightly to the stability of the highest mind, then freed from motion, it also surpasses the necessity of fate. Therefore as reasoning is to knowing, as becoming is to being, as time is to eternity, and as a circle is to the center, so is the moving course of fate to the unmoving simplicity of providence.

"That course of fate moves heaven and the stars; it mixes together in harmony the elements and transforms them by changing them one into another. It renews all things that are born and die through the growth of their offspring and seed from generation to generation. It also ties together the actions and

Haec actus etiam fortunasque hominum indissolubili causarum conexione constringit, quae cum ab immobilis providentiae proficiscatur exordiis, ipsas quoque immutabiles esse necesse est. Ita enim res optime reguntur, si manens in divina mente simplicitas indeclinabilem causarum ordinem promat. Hic vero ordo res mutabiles et alioquin temere fluituras propria incommutabilitate coerceat.

"Quo fit ut tametsi vobis hunc ordinem minime considerare valentibus confusa omnia perturbataque videantur, nihilo minus tamen suus modus ad bonum dirigens cuncta disponat. Nihil est enim quod mali causa ne ab ipsis quidem improbis fiat; quos, ut uberrime demonstratum est, bonum quaerentes pravus error avertit, nedum ordo de summi boni cardine proficiscens a suo quoquam deflectat exordio.

"Quae vero, inquies, potest ulla iniquior esse confusio, quam ut bonis tum adversa tum prospera, malis etiam tum optata tum odiosa contingant? Num igitur ea mentis integritate homines degunt, ut

fortunes of all mortals in an unbreakable chain of causes. And since these causes spring from the unchangeable beginnings of providence, it's necessary that they are unchanging as well. For it is in this way that things are governed best, if the simplicity remaining constant in the divine mind produces an unchangeable order of causes. And this order constrains by its own immutability changeable things that would otherwise flow forth randomly.

"And so it is that although everything may seem confused and out of place to you humans since you're not at all able to comprehend this order, nonetheless the individual workings of all things order them and direct them toward the good. For remember there is nothing done for the sake of evil, not even by wicked people. As we have abundantly demonstrated, it is immoral error that turns them aside as they are seeking good. Certainly it's not the order proceeding from the center point of the highest good that goes astray from its own starting point.

"But, you will ask, what confusion could possibly be more unfair than when good people have things turn out well sometimes and badly sometimes, while bad people sometimes gain what they hope for and other times get what they detest? But do humans really live with such infallible minds that

quos probos improbosve censuerunt eos quoque uti existimant esse necesse sit? Atqui in hoc hominum iudicia depugnant, et quos alii praemio alii supplicio dignos arbitrantur.

"Sed concedamus ut aliquis possit bonos malosque discernere; num igitur poterit intueri illam intimam temperiem, velut in corporibus dici solet, animorum? Non enim dissimile est miraculum nescienti cur sanis corporibus his quidem dulcia illis vero amara conveniant, cur aegri etiam quidam lenibus quidam vero acribus adiuventur. At hoc medicus, qui sanitatis ipsius atque aegritudinis modum temperamentumque dinoscit, minime miratur. Quid vero aliud animorum salus videtur esse quam probitas? Quid aegritudo quam vitia? Quis autem alius vel servator bonorum vel malorum depulsor quam rector ac medicator mentium deus? Qui cum ex alta providentiae specula respexit, quid unicuique conveniat agnoscit et quod convenire novit accommodat. Hic iam fit illud fatalis ordinis insigne miraculum, cum ab sciente geritur quod stupeant ignorantes.

"Nam ut pauca quae ratio valet humana de divina profunditate perstringam, de hoc quem tu iustissi-

those things they judge to be good or bad necessarily are that way? And of course different people judge these things in different ways so that those whom some think worthy of reward, others think worthy of punishment.

"But let's grant that someone is able to tell good and bad people apart. Do you think that person can look into another's inmost temperament,[14] to borrow a term from speaking about the body? It's not really different from when someone doesn't know why, in the case of healthy bodies, sweet things are right for some and sour things for others, or why some people are helped by gentle remedies and others by harsher medicines. But a physician, who is able to distinguish the workings of health and sickness, isn't amazed at all. Indeed what is the health of minds but goodness? What is sickness except evil? And who else is the preserver of good things and the remover of evil except God, the ruler and healer of minds. He looks out from the high watchtower of his providence and knows what is appropriate for each one and supplies each with what he knows is proper. Here the marvelous workings of fate are played out, when the one who knows accomplishes things that amaze those who don't know.

"For if I may, let me touch upon a few things concerning the depth of God that human reason might be strong enough to understand. A man you

mum et aequi servantissimum putas omnia scienti providentiae diversum videtur; et victricem quidem causam dis, victam vero Catoni placuisse familiaris noster Lucanus admonuit. Hic igitur quidquid citra spem videas geri, rebus quidem rectus ordo est, opinioni vero tuae perversa confusio. Sed sit aliquis ita bene moratus ut de eo divinum iudicium pariter et humanum consentiat, sed est animi viribus infirmus; cui si quid eveniat adversi, desinet colere forsitan innocentiam per quam non potuit retinere fortunam. Parcit itaque sapiens dispensatio ei quem deteriorem facere possit adversitas, ne cui non convenit, laborare patiatur. Est alius cunctis virtutibus absolutus sanctusque ac deo proximus; hunc contingi quibuslibet adversis nefas providentia iudicat adeo ut ne corporeis quidem morbis agitari sinat. Nam ut quidam me quoque excellentior:

> Ἀνδρὸς δὴ ἱεροῦ δέμας αἰθέρες ᾠκοδόμησαν.

Fit autem saepe, uti bonis summa rerum regenda deferatur, ut exuberans retundatur improbitas. Aliis

think to be most just and the greatest servant of what is right, providence, knowing all, might look upon differently. Our student Lucan warned us that the conqueror's cause pleased the gods, but Cato's was pleasing to the conquered.[15] Whatever you might see happen in this world against your expectation does indeed follow the right order of things, though in your opinion it all seems perversely confused. But suppose there were someone so excellent in character that both divine and human judgment agreed about him. Now suppose this same man was weak in the strength of his spirit, so that if adverse events happened to him, he would perhaps lack the ability to preserve his innocence by which good fortune had been granted to him. So a wise dispensation might spare him, since adversity would weaken him, and not allow him to be oppressed by events he couldn't overcome. Another man might be perfect in his virtues, holy and near to God, and thus providence might judge it wrong to allow him to suffer any adversities at all, so that he's not even troubled by bodily ailments. As someone more excellent than me once said:

Heavenly powers did build the body of a holy man.[16]

But it often happens that the highest power of ruling is given to good people so that uncontrolled wickedness

mixta quaedam pro animorum qualitate distribuit; quosdam remordet ne longa felicitate luxurient, alios duris agitariut virtutes animi patientiae usu atque exercitatione confirment. Alii plus aequo metuunt quod ferre possunt, alii plus aequo despiciunt quod ferre non possunt; hos in experimentum sui tristibus ducit. Nonnulli venerandum saeculi nomen gloriosae pretio mortis emerunt: quidam suppliciis inexpugnabiles exemplum ceteris praetulerunt invictam malis esse virtutem. Quae quam recte atque disposite et ex eorum bono quibus accedere videntur fiant, nulla dubitatio est.

"Nam illud quoque, quod improbis nunc tristia nunc optata proveniunt, ex eisdem ducitur causis; ac de tristibus quidem nemo miratur, quod eos male meritos omnes existimant. Quorum quidem supplicia tum ceteros ab sceleribus deterrent, tum ipsos quibus invehuntur emendant; laeta vero magnum bonis argumentum loquuntur, quid de huiusmodi felicitate debeant iudicare quam famulari saepe improbis cernant. In qua re illud etiam dispensari credo, quod est forsitan alicuius tam praeceps atque inportuna natura ut eum in scelera potius exacerbare possit rei familiaris inopia; huius morbo providentia

may be restrained. To some providence distributes a mixture of good and evil according to the qualities of their minds. Others it restrains so they don't luxuriate in their happiness too long. Some it torments with hardships to strengthen the virtues of their minds and build up their patience by practice. Some are too fearful of what they might be able to endure, while others aren't fearful enough of what they in fact can't bear and so providence teaches them by trial. Some have purchased an enduring name in this world at the price of a glorious death. Others have endured torments and shown the rest of humanity an example of virtue unconquered by evil. There is no doubt that these things are done justly and in proper order for the good of those to whom they happen.

"And it's also true and springs from the same causes that things hoped for as well as harsh things happen to the wicked. No one wonders at the fact that harsh things happen to bad people since everyone thinks they merit their torments and because their punishments deter others from doing evil deeds and correct those people who suffer them. On the other hand, the fortunate things that happen to bad people makes a powerful argument for good people to hear regarding how they should judge this kind of prosperity they so often see befall the wicked. I think in these cases it's also arranged that

collatae pecuniae remedio medetur. Hic foedatam probris conscientiam exspectans et se cum fortuna sua comparans, forsitan pertimescit ne cuius ei iucundus usus est, sit tristis amissio. Mutabit igitur mores ac dum fortunam metuit amittere, nequitiam derelinquit. Alios in cladem meritam praecipitavit indigne acta felicitas; quibusdam permissum puniendi ius, ut exercitii bonis et malis esset causa supplicii. Nam ut probis atque improbis nullum foedus est, ita ipsi inter se improbi nequeunt convenire. Quidni, cum a semet ipsis discerpentibus conscientiam vitiis quisque dissentiat faciantque saepe, quae cum gesserint non fuisse gerenda decernant?

"Ex quo saepe summa illa providentia protulit insigne miraculum, ut malos mali bonos facerent. Nam dum iniqua sibi a pessimis quidam perpeti videntur, noxiorum odio flagrantes ad virtutis frugem rediere, dum se eis dissimiles student esse quos oderant. Sola est enim divina vis cui mala quoque bona sint, cum eis competenter utendo alicuius boni elicit effectum. Ordo enim quidam cuncta complectitur, ut quod adsignata ordinis ratione decesserit,

if someone has a headstrong and impulsive nature so that a lack of wealth might be able to drive him to crime, providence treats this disease by providing him money. Then there's another person who, examining his conscience fouled by wicked deeds and comparing his evil actions with his good fortune, grows fearful that losing the things so pleasing to him would make him sad. He therefore changes his ways because he's afraid of losing his good fortune and so gives up his wickedness. Some people have been cast down into well-deserved disaster by misused good fortune. Some people are granted the right to punish others so that they may be the cause of training for the good or chastisement for the wicked. For just as there is no agreement between the righteous and the unrighteous, so too the unrighteous can never agree among themselves. And how could they? Each disagrees even within himself while their vices tear them apart, so that they often do wicked acts they later realize they never should have done.

"And so it is that the highest providence often produces the remarkable wonder that evil people make other evil people good. For some evil people, when they think they are suffering injustice at the hands of people much worse than themselves, burn with anger against those injuring them and return to virtue because they don't want to be like the men they hate. But only to the divine power can evil things also be good, since by using them carefully

hoc licet in alium, tamen ordinem relabatur, ne quid in regno providentiae liceat temeritati.

‘Αργαλέον δέ με ταῦτα θεὸν ὣς πάντ’ ἀγορεύειν.

Neque enim fas est homini cunctas divinae operae machinas vel ingenio comprehendere vel explicare sermone. Hoc tantum perspexisse sufficiat, quod naturarum omnium proditor deus idem ad bonum dirigens cuncta disponat, dumque ea quae protulit in sui similitudinem retinere festinat, malum omne de reipublicae suae terminis per fatalis seriem necessitatis eliminet. Quo fit ut quae in terris abundare creduntur, si disponentem providentiam spectes, nihil usquam mali esse perpendas.

"Sed video te iam dudum et pondere quaestionis oneratum et rationis prolixitate fatigatum aliquam carminis exspectare dulcedinem. Accipe igitur haustum quo refectus firmior in ulteriora contendas.

it produces some good from the end result. For a certain order embraces all things, so that even when something has slipped away from the orderly rule assigned to it, yet it slips into another that is ordered still, so that nothing in the kingdom of providence is random.

> *But it isn't right for me to talk about these things as if I were a god.*[17]

It isn't permitted for mortals to understand all the machines of the divine work in their minds nor to express them in words. Let it suffice to understand that God, as author of all of nature, governs all things and directs them to good. And while he hastens to maintain those things he has created in his own image, he banishes every evil from the borders of his kingdom by the course of necessary fate. So it happens that if you were able to see through the eyes of providence at all things believed so abundant on earth, you would judge that there is no evil in the world.

"But I see that you're weighed down by the burden of this inquiry and exhausted by the length of the argument, so that you're looking forward to a sweet song. So take now a drink and once you've been refreshed, you can press forward a stronger man.

"Iamne igitur vides quid haec omnia quae diximus consequatur?"

"Quidnam?" inquam.

"Omnem," inquit, "bonam prorsus esse fortunam."

"Et qui id," inquam, "fieri potest?"

"Attende," inquit. "Cum omnis fortuna vel iucunda vel aspera tum remunerandi exercendive bonos tum puniendi corrigendive improbos causa deferatur, omnis bona quam vel iustam constat esse vel utilem."

"Nimis quidem," inquam, "vera ratio etsi quam paulo ante docuisti providentiam fatumve considerem, firmis viribus nixa sententia. Sed eam si placet inter eas quas inopinabiles paulo ante posuisti numeremus."

"Qui?" inquit.

"Quia id hominum sermo communis usurpat et quidem crebro quorundam malam esse fortunam."

"Visne igitur," inquit, "paulisper vulgi sermonibus accedamus, ne nimium velut ab humanitatis usu recessisse videamur?"

"Ut placet," inquam.

All Fortune Is Good

"Now do you see the conclusion we can draw from all we've said?"

"What is that?" I asked.

"That all fortune," she said, "is certainly good."

"But how," I asked, "can that possibly be?"

"Listen to me," she said. "Since every kind of fortune, whether delightful or bitter, is given for the purpose of rewarding or teaching good people or punishing or correcting bad people, every kind of fortune must be good since we agree it is just or useful."

"That is painfully true," I said. "And if I think about providence or fate that we talked about just a little while ago, it's clear that your conclusion is strongly and firmly reasoned. But if it's acceptable to you, may we number it among the conclusions you put forward a short time ago as impossible to believe?"

"Why?" she asked.

"Because it's a common expression, used often by many, that some people have bad fortune."

"So," she said, "you want us for a little while to use the language of the common crowd so that we don't seem to stray too far from everyday speech?"

"If it pleases you," I said.

"Nonne igitur bonum censes esse quod prodest?"

"Ita est," inquam.

"Quae vero aut exercet aut corrigit, prodest?"

"Fateor," inquam.

"Bona igitur?"

"Quidni."

"Sed haec eorum est qui vel in virtute positi contra aspera bellum gerunt, vel a vitiis declinantes virtutis iter arripiunt."

"Negare," inquam, "nequeo."

"Quid vero iucunda, quae in praemium tribuitur bonis, num vulgus malam esse decernit?"

"Nequaquam; verum uti est ita quoque esse optimam censet."

"Quid reliqua, quae cum sit aspera, iusto supplicio malos coercet, num bonam populus putat?"

"Immo omnium," inquam, "quae excogitari possunt, iudicat esse miserrimam."

"Vide igitur ne opinionem populi sequentes quiddam valde inopinabile confecerimus."

"Quid?" inquam.

"Well then, don't you think that whatever is to someone's advantage is also good?"

"Yes," I said.

"And what instructs or corrects is also advantageous?"

"Indeed it is," I said.

"And therefore good?"

"Of course."

"These things apply to those already grounded in virtue who wage war against adversity or to those are turning away from vices and undertaking the journey toward virtue."

"I can't deny that," I said.

"But what about pleasant fortune that's given as a reward to good people—do the common people think that's bad?"

"Not at all. They think it to be the very best fortune, which it is."

"What about the other kind of fortune, which, although harsh, constrains wicked people by punishment. The common people don't think that's good, do they?"

"No indeed," I said, "they judge it to be the worst kind of fortune anyone could imagine."

"Be careful then, for by following the opinion of the common people it seems we've reached a very surprising conclusion."

"What is that?" I asked.

"Ex his enim," ait, "quae concessa sunt, evenit eorum quidem qui vel sunt vel in possessione vel in provectu vel in adeptione virtutis, omnem quaecumque sit bonam, in improbitate vero manentibus omnem pessimam esse fortunam."

"Hoc," inquam, "verum est, tametsi nemo audeat confiteri."

"Quare," inquit, "ita vir sapiens moleste ferre non debet, quotiens in fortunae certamen adducitur, ut virum fortem non decet indignari, quotiens increpuit bellicus tumultus; utrique enim, huic quidem gloriae propagandae illi vero conformandae sapientiae, difficultas ipsa materia est. Ex quo etiam virtus vocatur quod suis viribus nitens non superetur adversis. Neque enim vos in provectu positi virtutis diffluere deliciis et emarcescere voluptate venistis. Proelium cum omni fortuna animis acre conseritis, ne vos aut tristis opprimat aut iucunda corrumpat. Firmis medium viribus occupate! Quidquid aut infra subsistit aut ultra progreditur, habet contemptum felicitatis, non habet praemium laboris. In vestra enim situm manu qualem vobis fortunam formare malitis; omnis enim quae videtur aspera nisi aut exercet aut corrigit punit."

"From these arguments," she said, "it turns out that for everyone who is in possession of virtue or who is moving toward it or beginning to gain virtue for themselves, all fortune is good. But for those who are immovable in their wickedness, every fortune is very bad."

"That is true," I said, "even if no one dares to agree."

"Because of this," she said, "a wise man ought not to be dismayed every time he is drawn into a struggle with misfortune, just as it wouldn't be fitting for a brave man to worry whenever he hears the clash of battle. For each of these men, the struggle is an opportunity, for the soldier to gain glory and for the wise man to increase his wisdom. For from this virtue gets its name, since by relying on its own strength it isn't overcome by adversity.[18] For those of you who remain firm on the path of virtue have not come this far to wallow in self-indulgence or dissipate yourselves in pleasure. You are engaged in a fierce battle of the mind with all kinds of fortune, lest the bad wear you down or the delightful corrupt you. Hold to the middle course with firm strength![19] Whoever halts before it or marches beyond it has contempt for happiness and no reward to show for his labors. In your own hands is placed the kind of fortune you wish to shape for yourselves, for every fortune that seems difficult will indeed punish you unless you see it as teaching or correcting you."

NOTES

Introduction

1 *The Discarded Image*, p. 78.

Book 1. A Visitor in Prison

1 The Latin meter here is elegiac couplets, common for mournful verse. This first poem is deliberately melodramatic and self-pitying to reflect the prisoner's state of mind (*heu* "alas").

2 Latin *Camenae*, the native Roman name for the Greek Muses.

3 Boethius is in fact only in his mid-forties.

4 Latin *fortuna* ("fortune, fate"), the first occurrence of this key word in the *Consolation.*

5 Boethius seems to be referring to the wax masks of their noble ancestors that Romans proudly displayed in the atrium of their homes. If neglected, they would become covered with soot from the hearth fire.

6 The Greek letter *Pi* (Π) stands for practical types of philosophy, while *Theta* (Θ) represents theoretical

philosophy. One must start at the lower but crucial level of practical before ascending the ladder to the higher realms of the theoretical.

7 Literally "on Eleatic and Academic philosophy." Parmenides (died c. 450 BCE) of Elea, a Greek colony in southern Italy, was a leading figure, along with his contemporary Zeno, of the Eleatic movement, which emphasized the singular, indestructible nature of reality and the need for discovering truth by reason rather than trusting the appearances of the senses. The Academics are named for the teachings of the Academy founded by Plato (died 347 BCE) in Athens and carried on by his followers.

8 In Greek mythology, bird-like women who lured sailors to their doom with enchanted song.

9 Remembering is a key concept in the *Consolation* and further developed later in the book. Boethius is drawing on the Platonic notion of anamnesis or recollection as a type of medicine for the troubled soul.

10 Just as Athena removes the mist from the eyes of Diomedes in the *Iliad* (5.127–28) and Venus clears the vision of Aeneas (*Aeneid* 2.604–6), in both cases to see the divine at work beyond the limits of human perception.

11 Socrates was executed by the Athenians in 399 BCE. Boethius here is borrowing from the language of Christian martyrdom.

12 The Epicurean and Stoic schools of thought arose about a century after the death of Socrates. Epicureans believed that detachment from the world and moderate

pleasure were the goals of life, while Stoics taught the importance of duty and wariness of emotions. Boethius was in fact deeply influenced by the Stoics, especially the Roman writer Seneca, and not entirely hostile to Epicurean teachings.

13 Anaxagoras (died 428 BCE) fled Athens after being charged with impiety. His contemporary Zeno of Elea was tortured to death for opposing tyranny. Canius was a Stoic philosopher killed by the Roman emperor Caligula about 40 CE. Both Seneca and Soranus were executed unjustly by the emperor Nero two decades later. Seneca was a tutor and advisor of Nero, a ruler Boethius uses several times in the *Consolation* as an example of an evil tyrant—a silent but unmistakable comparison to the Ostrogothic ruler Theoderic who had imprisoned him.

14 Boethius uses the original Greek a number of times in the *Consolation*.

15 A Greek proverb for a person too dull-witted to understand something.

16 *Iliad* 1.363. These are the words the goddess Thetis says to her tearful son Achilles after he has been mistreated by the king Agamemnon.

17 Plato says in his *Republic* (5.473D) that the best state is one in which philosophers rule as kings.

18 We know little of Conigastus or Trigguilla except that they were Goths in the service of Theoderic. Boethius in fact had more serious difficulties with his fellow

Romans in royal service than he did with the Goths in court.

19 Latin *coemptio* was a compulsory sale of grain to the state at a below-market price. This was in addition to any ordinary taxation.

20 Campania was an agriculturally rich province around the Bay of Naples in southern Italy, where many of the estates were owned by the Roman senatorial class. The date of this event is not known, but it probably occurred while Boethius was master of the offices under Theoderic. The Praetorian prefect was originally the head of the Roman emperor's bodyguard, but by this time the office was similar to that of a prime minister with control over revenue and expenditures. He would have been a native Roman like Boethius.

21 Paulinus was consul in 498, while Albinus had held that rank five years earlier. Albinus was charged with treason after he wrote a letter supporting the eastern emperor Justin. Cyprian, a Roman nobleman devoted to the service of Theoderic, accused Albinus and then Boethius of conspiring against the king, a charge that was the beginning of Boethius's downfall.

22 Latin *aula*: "court, palace," originally from the Greek word for a forecourt of a house, thus *apud aulicos* "people of the *aula*, courtiers."

23 Basilius, Opilio, and Gaudentius were all Roman senators serving in the court of Theoderic. Opilio was the

son-in-law of Basilius and brother to Cyprian, the Gothic loyalist mentioned above as another accuser of Boethius.

24 The ancient practice of seeking holy sanctuary in a temple of the gods carried over to Christian churches.

25 In what must have been a bitter blow for Boethius, the Roman Senate he was working so hard to protect passed a resolution condemning him, thus distancing themselves from his actions in hope of saving themselves from the wrath of Theoderic.

26 Plato *Theaetetus* 151D.

27 The source of this quotation is unknown, but it has been attributed to Epicurus or a later commentary on Plato.

28 Theoderic held court at several cities in northern Italy aside from his capital at Ravenna.

29 In Pavia, south of Milan. The Roman mile was slightly shorter than the English mile.

30 Latin *sacrilegium* has a wide range of meanings, including "robbery" or "destruction of a temple and defiling religious rites," but it is clear in this context that Boethius is referring to black magic. A dozen years before his imprisonment, two Roman senators had been executed for allegedly using such magic, forbidden in Christian Italy.

31 The famous Greek philosopher (died c. 495 BCE) who used mathematics to explain the order of the universe, a concept important to Boethius.

32 Latin *maleficium* was often used specifically for sorcery and black magic, unlike *sacrilegium* above, which can have a broader meaning.

33 The interest Boethius took in astronomical phenomena seems to have made such charges more credible in the eyes of those who saw little difference between science and sorcery.

34 Literally "While I was barking out."

35 Homer *Iliad* 2.204. These are the words Odysseus speaks to the Greek soldiers to stop a mutiny against King Agamemnon.

36 A Stoic idea that true freedom consists of following the path of virtue, not doing whatever one might wish (Seneca *Dialogues* 7.15.7: "We have been born into a kingdom. To obey God is liberty"). Later Christian writers such as Augustine embraced this idea.

37 Latin *attingere*: a medical term used for a physician taking the pulse of a patient.

38 Literally "by what rudders do you think it is steered?"

Book 2. Fortune Is Never Constant

1 Latin *fucos*: literally "dyes, paints," but comes to mean "deceptions, deceits, tricks."

2 Latin *adytum*: in origin a Greek word meaning "the innermost shrine or sanctuary of a temple."

3 Latin *numen* can be translated "goddess" but it also has a more primal meaning of "divine power, supernatural force."

4 That is, if you had been thinking about Fortune properly.

5 The wheel of Fortune is an idea found in classical authors long before Boethius, but the *Consolation* made it one of the most famous images of medieval literature and art.

6 The story in Herodotus (1.86–87) tells how the powerful Lydian ruler Croesus was defeated by the great king Cyrus of Persia but ultimately pardoned after telling Cyrus that there is a turning wheel of Fortune in human affairs that allows no man to be on top forever.

7 Paullus was a former Roman consul and general who in the second century BCE defeated Perseus, last of the Macedonian kings (Livy 45.8).

8 Homer *Iliad* 24.527. Achilles speaks these words to the mourning King Priam of Troy.

9 Philosophy is here using a rhetorical device called *praeteritio* ("passing over"), mentioning something she claims she wasn't going to mention at all.

10 In 522, the two sons of Boethius, named Boethius and Symmachus, were made joint consuls in Rome. Boethius's arrest and downfall came soon after.

11 The Circus Maximus beneath the Palatine Hill in Rome was the site of the expensive games and shows sponsored by new consuls and their families.

12 Latin *calculum ponere*: literally "to put the stone on the counting board," an ancient way of reckoning debts.

13 A famous line of the *Consolation* echoed by Dante (*Inferno* 5.121–23): "There is no greater pain than to remember a time when you were happy, while plunged in misery."

14 Soon after Boethius's death, Symmachus was arrested and executed by Theoderic.

15 Rusticiana survived the purges of her husband and father. When Byzantine forces invaded Rome years later, she had all the statues of Theoderic smashed in revenge.

16 Boethius's sons were not marked for death by Theoderic like their father and grandfather. They became leading citizens of Rome and in decades to come Boethius's descendants flourished in both Italy and Constantinople.

17 Christian readers would have seen this as a reference to holy martyrs, but Boethius is probably referring to the suffering and death of persecuted pagan philosophers, such as Socrates and Seneca.

18 Latin *famulus* can be a free servant or attendant but is often a slave.

19 "Know thyself" (Greek *gnothi seauton*) was the famous saying inscribed on Apollo's temple at Delphi (Plato *Protagoras* 343B).

20 Juvenal *Satire* 10.22: *cantabit vacuus coram latrone viator* ("the empty-handed traveler will sing before a thief").

21 Literally "Etnas" (plural of the Sicilian volcano Etna).

22 The Roman Republic empowered the tribunes of the people to check (but not eliminate) the power of the two consuls, the annually elected chief executives of the state. In 509 BCE, the Romans had expelled their last king, Tarquin the Proud, and in the centuries after despised the name *rex* ("king").

23 Boethius doesn't name the characters in the story, but he may be referring to Zeno, mentioned earlier.

24 Busiris was an Egyptian king who sacrificed one guest each year to Zeus until he foolishly chose the wandering Hercules as his victim.

25 The Roman general Regulus fought against the Carthaginians in the First Punic War, but was captured and released on his promise that he would return to Carthage to face death if he did not persuade the Senate to accept a truce. He argued against the truce in Rome, then faithfully returned to Carthage for execution.

26 Boethius is drawing extensively on Cicero's *Dream of Scipio* (book 6 of his *Republic*) in this section, an imaginary journey in which the deceased Roman general Scipio takes his adoptive grandson of the same name to the heavens to view the earth from above. Boethius is also using the commentary on the work by the fifth-century CE scholar Macrobius.

27 Ptolemy was an astronomer and geographer who worked in Alexandria in the second century CE. He

argued that the sphere of the earth was divided into frozen zones around the north and south poles and burning lands around the equator, leaving only about a quarter of the planet on which people might live.

28 Latin *saeptum*: a small pen often used for farm animals.

29 The Romans had a clear geographical picture of the Mediterranean, Near East, and western Europe but only a progressively vaguer idea of Africa below the Sahara, Asia east of the Indus River, and northern Europe beyond the Rhine. They of course knew nothing of the lands across the Atlantic.

30 Cicero *Republic* 6.22 (Macrobius *Commentary* 2.10). The Caucasus are a mountain range between the Black Sea and the Caspian Sea. The Parthians or Persians bordered the Roman Empire on the east in modern-day Iran.

31 That is, before Boethius's fall from power.

Book 3. True Happiness

1 Boethius uses Latin *felicitas* ("happiness") carefully since it can be either true or false. For a higher state of unqualified happiness, he will often use *beatitudo* ("true happiness, blessedness, joy").

2 A reference to Plato's Allegory of the Cave, in which prisoners sit chained and immobile in a cave so they see only shadows on a wall.

3 *causa* is deleted by some editors.

4 Aristotle *Nicomachean Ethics* 8; Cicero *On Friendship*.

5 Epicurus of Samos (died 270 BCE) was a materialist philosopher who taught that the pursuit of pleasure allowed people to live free from fear and worry, but he also believed unrestrained physical pleasure was undesirable and diminished a person's happiness.

6 Boethius is using the language of Plato to express that the ultimate goal all humans seek is the Good—an idea that transcends whatever various means (wealth, power, etc.) we may use to try to obtain it.

7 Latin *struma*: "a tumor, blister, wart." Catullus 52.2. Nothing else is known about Nonius.

8 We know little of Decoratus, who served as a quaestor under Theoderic.

9 Latin *umbratiles*: "shadowy, in the shade." The high offices are shadowy not in the sense that they are unseen or obscure but because of their nature as mere shadows or dim reflections of true worthiness, like the shadows in Plato's cave.

10 A praetor was once an important Roman magistrate, but by the time of Boethius the office was seen by many senators as a ceremonial and financially burdensome duty best avoided.

11 The prefect of the public grain supply (*annona*) was a crucial and honored role in earlier Roman history, but in the turmoil of late antiquity, assuring adequate

grain shipments to Rome from Sicily or Africa was an increasingly difficult and thankless task.

12 Boethius is pointedly criticizing himself as one who had enjoyed friendship with a king, Theoderic, who turned on him and sentenced him to death.

13 King Dionysius I of Syracuse in Sicily showed his guest Damocles what it was like to be a king by hanging a sword suspended only by a thread over his head during a great banquet.

14 Nero ordered his advisor Seneca to commit suicide in 65 CE. The emperor Antoninus (known as Caracalla) executed the famous Roman jurist Papinianus, who had also once been his tutor, in 212 CE.

15 Euripides *Andromache* 319–20.

16 A biting critique given that pride in one's family name and lineage was of enormous importance to Romans throughout their history, including to Boethius.

17 Euripides *Andromache* 418–20.

18 Wealth, honors, power, fame, pleasure.

19 From a lost work of Aristotle. Lynceus was one of the Argonauts who sailed with Jason and had proverbially keen sight. Alcibiades, a contemporary of Socrates, was an Athenian military leader who was considered the most handsome man of his age.

20 This section marks a turning point in the *Consolation*. With the false pathways to happiness now examined and dismissed, the discovery of true happiness can begin. What before had mainly been Philosophy lecturing the

prisoner now becomes more of a Socratic dialogue between her and Boethius.

21 Plato *Timaeus* 27C.

22 A Greek *porisma* (plural *porismata*) is a by-product of a logical argument, which Boethius translates using Latin *corollarium* ("little gift"), a kind of bonus to the previous conclusion.

23 That people may become gods by participating in the divine nature may seem odd since by definition a monotheistic God is singular. But it is an idea that has Platonic, Neoplatonic, and earlier Christian origins (e.g., John 10:34–35; 2 Peter 1:4). It became an important idea in Christian theology, especially in the Eastern Orthodox Church.

24 Latin *medulla* is used for both the marrow of bones in animals and the pith or spongy cellular tissue in the interior of the stems and branches of trees.

25 Boethius here lists the four traditional elements of fire, earth, air, and water.

26 Latin *nota*: "token, sign, mark."

27 That is, when he was born into a human body and forgot his heavenly knowledge.

28 One of the few clear biblical references in the *Consolation* (Wisdom 8:1).

29 Stories of the giants fighting against the gods go back to Hesiod's *Theogony*, but Boethius is perhaps thinking of Ovid *Metamorphoses* 1.151–60. The giants are proverbial examples of hybris and resistance to the divine order of the universe.

30 Augustine *Confessions* 7.12.

31 Fragment 8.43, quoted by Plato (*Sophist* 244E).

32 *Timaeus* 29B.

Book 4. How Can Evil Go Unpunished?

1 Latin *paterfamilias*: the ancient Roman title for the father of a household who held absolute power over his home and family.

2 Virgil *Aeneid* 12.764–65.

3 *Gorgias* 466.

4 A crown of leaves was often the prize for victory in ancient athletic contests. It was also a popular metaphor for the reward of the Christian life (1 Corinthians 9:24–25).

5 Literally "turned face to face."

6 Boethius is capable of wonderful irony and subtle humor in the *Consolation*. We should always keep in mind the context of his writing this work, that he is being unjustly punished and soon to be executed by Theodoric, a very powerful and, in Boethius's mind, a very evil man. The phrase "and perhaps sooner than you might wish" in Philosophy's reply suggests Boethius's eminent death and the fact that he will then be beyond the reach of evil men.

7 This is likely a reference not to the Christian doctrine of Purgatory but to the teachings of Plato (*Gorgias* 524–27).

8 This line is not in the manuscripts but has been added by editors so that the text makes sense.

9 *lex* ("law") in most manuscripts but corrected to *nex* ("death, execution") by most editors.

10 The hydra was a fierce, multiheaded monster Hercules battled, but as he cut off one head, two more grew in its place. He was finally able to stop the heads from growing back when he cauterized the wounds with fire.

11 That is, it will be some time before there is another poetry section since this is the longest prose chapter in the *Consolation*.

12 Latin *anima* ("soul, spirit") here is likely referring to the Platonic and especially Neoplatonic concept of world soul, the animating power of the universe, a force lower and distinct from God.

13 Although familiar from Christian theology, Platonists, Stoics, and Neoplatonists also believed in a number of varied intermediate and superhuman forces used by God to govern the universe, including angels and demons.

14 Latin *temperies* ("temperament, mixture of substances") is a medical term drawing on the ancient and medieval belief that health derives from a proper balance of qualities in the body.

15 *Pharsalia* 1.128. Lucan was a first-century CE Roman writer who composed an epic poem about the civil war between Julius Caesar and his senatorial opponents,

including Cato, considered by many to be more virtuous than the victorious Caesar.

16 Source unknown, but perhaps from a late Neoplatonic commentary.

17 Homer *Iliad* 12.176.

18 Boethius is making a pun here saying that *virtus* ("virtue") is derived from the similar word *vires* ("strength"). But as he probably knew from reading Cicero (*Tusculan Disputations* 2.43) if nothing else, *virtus* in fact comes from *vir* ("man").

19 The Aristotelean ideal of virtue as the mean between extremes (*Nicomachean Ethics* 1115A).

FURTHER READING

Bieler, Ludwig, ed. *Anicii Manlii Severini Boethii Philosophiae Consolatio*, Corpus Christianorum, Series Latina XCIV. Turnhout: Brepols, 1984.

Blackwood, Stephen. *The Consolation of Boethius as Poetic Liturgy*. Oxford: Oxford University Press, 2022.

Burns, Thomas. *A History of the Ostrogoths*. Bloomington: Indiana University Press, 1991.

Chadwick, Henry. *Boethius: The Consolations of Music, Logic, Theology, and Philosophy*. Oxford: Oxford University Press, 1998.

Cooper, Lane. *A Concordance of Boethius: The Five Theological Tractates and the Consolation of Philosophy*. Cambridge, Mass.: The Mediaeval Academy of America, 1911.

Donato, Antonio. *Boethius' Consolation of Philosophy as a Product of Late Antiquity*. London: Bloomsbury, 2013.

Gibson, Margaret, ed. *Boethius: His Life, Thought, and Influence*. Oxford: Basil Blackwell, 1981.

Goins, Scott, and Barbara H. Wyman, eds. *Boethius: The Consolation of Philosophy*. San Francisco: Ignatius Press, 2012.

Halporn, James W., Martin Ostwald, and Thomas G. Rosenmayer. *The Meters of Greek and Latin Poetry*. Indianapolis: Hackett Publishing Company, 1994.

Lewis, C. S. *The Discarded Image: An Introduction to Medieval and Renaissance Literature*. Cambridge: Cambridge University Press, 1964.

Marenbon, John. *Boethius*. Oxford: Oxford University Press, 2003.

——, ed. *The Cambridge Companion to Boethius*. Cambridge: Cambridge University Press, 2009.

Moorhead, John. *Theoderic in Italy*. Oxford: Clarendon Press, 1992.

Moreschini, Claudio, ed. *Boethius: De Consolatione Philosophiae et Opuscula Theologica*. Berlin: De Gruyter, 2005.

O'Donnell, James J., ed. *Boethius: Consolatio Philosophiae*. Bryn Mawr: Bryn Mawr Commentaries, 1990.

Relihan, Joel C., trans. *Boethius: Consolation of Philosophy*. Indianapolis: Hackett Publishing Company, 2001.

——. *The Prisoner's Philosophy: Life and Death in Boethius's Consolation*. Notre Dame: University of Notre Dame Press, 2007.

Sharples, R. W., ed. *Cicero: On Fate and Boethius: The Consolation of Philosophy*. Oxford: Oxbow University Press, 1992.

Stewart, H. F., E. K. Rand, and S. J. Tester, eds. *Boethius: The Theological Tractates and the Consolation of Phi-*

losophy. Loeb Classical Library vol. 74. Cambridge, Mass.: Harvard University Press, 1973.

Walsh, P. G., trans. *Boethius: The Consolation of Philosophy*. Oxford: Oxford University Press, 1999.

Watts, Victor, trans. *Boethius: The Consolation of Philosophy*. New York: Penguin Books, 1999.

Wickham, Chris. *Early Medieval Italy: Central Power and Local Society 400–1000*. Ann Arbor: University of Michigan Press, 1990.

Wiemer, Hans-Ulrich. *Theoderic the Great: King of Goths, Ruler of Romans*. New Haven: Yale University Press, 2023.